I0423563

Safety and Soundness

Capital Adequacy (C)	Asset Quality (A)	Management (M)	Earnings (E)	Liquidity (L)	Sensitivity to Market Risk (S)	Other Activities (O)

Oil and Gas Production Lending

April 2014

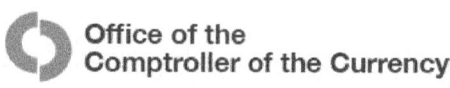

Office of the Comptroller of the Currency

Washington, DC 20219

Contents

Introduction

The Office of the Comptroller of the Currency's (OCC) *Comptroller's Handbook* booklet, "Oil and Gas Production Lending," provides guidance for bank examiners and bankers on the risks presented by oil and natural gas (O&G) production lending activities. The booklet is one of several specialized lending booklets and augments guidance contained in the "Loan Portfolio Management," "Large Bank Supervision," and "Community Bank Supervision" booklets of the *Comptroller's Handbook*.

The booklet addresses the risks inherent in O&G lending and describes supervisory expectations and regulatory requirements for prudent risk management of this lending activity. The booklet includes expanded examination procedures to guide examiners in evaluating the impact of O&G lending activities on the risk profile and financial condition of a bank.

Throughout this booklet, national banks and federal savings associations are referred to collectively as banks, except when it is necessary to distinguish between the two. The glossary in appendix C contains definitions of technical terms used in the booklet.

Overview

Major segments of the O&G industry include exploration and production (upstream); gathering, processing, and transportation of oil or natural gas (midstream); and refining, marketing, and distribution (downstream). Loans to downstream companies generally are structured similar to other commercial and industrial loans.[1] Industry participants include international integrated O&G companies, U.S. integrated O&G companies, exploration and production companies, refining and marketing firms, drilling companies, and service businesses. U.S. integrated O&G companies explore for and develop O&G worldwide, but their refining and marketing operations are generally limited to the United States. This booklet addresses only the more specialized exploration and production (E&P) segment of the industry.

Business Description

Also known as major oil companies, or majors, international integrated O&G companies are involved in almost every aspect of the O&G business: upstream, midstream, and downstream. Most are also engaged in the manufacture and sale of petrochemicals. International integrated O&G companies conduct their operations worldwide and are among

---

[1] Services provided to producers by the midstream firms include transportation, gathering, processing, and storage for natural gas, oil, and refined products. Borrowing entities are often structured as master limited partnerships, which provide tax advantages for their partners. Refining, marketing, and distribution companies (downstream) refine and sell crude oil products such as gasoline, jet fuel, heating oil, motor oil, and various lubricants. The location and state of industry infrastructure and changing technology sometimes have a significant impact on production costs, commodity prices, and profitability, which may then affect exploration and production (upstream) companies.

the largest and most recognized firms in the world. The largest such firms are known as the super majors.

Smaller E&P companies are called independents because they are not associated with any of the major O&G companies. Some of these independent E&P companies have evolved from spin-offs of larger corporations, such as railroads, integrated O&G companies, pipeline companies, or utilities. A number of companies began with a single O&G field and grew by acquiring smaller competitors or individual properties from larger competitors.

Commodity price volatility presents risk to all O&G companies over time. As a result of this risk, profitability can be volatile and the industry generally poses higher credit risk than most other sectors without strong lending controls. Diversification sometimes allows large majors and super majors to manage risks and reduce profit volatility more easily than independents. Since natural gas is difficult and costly to export, natural gas markets are continental, so price volatility within each geographic market is driven by events within that continent. The crude oil market, on the other hand, is global, so geopolitical risks have a greater potential effect on companies with drilling and extraction operations overseas. North American natural gas is a commodity in which the independent E&P companies have historically been cost competitive, due to lack of competition from low-cost imports. Independents are key players in North American natural gas and oil. Independents tend to be more concentrated than majors but also have more flexibility in making strategic decisions. This flexibility sometimes gives independents the ability to produce O&G at a lower cost than larger competitors do. In addition to their exposure to commodity price volatility, O&G businesses have other differences from most companies in other sectors.

Unlike most companies, which increase assets as they grow, O&G reserves deplete as the company sells O&G over time. Because reserves are usually the company's largest asset, the company has to replace reserves or it will eventually become unprofitable. To sustain profitable production, E&P companies have to replace reserves at a reasonable cost. As a result, exploration and development often compose a large portion of an E&P company's expenditures. Exploration, however, does not always result in successful replacement, and some types of exploratory drilling, such as deepwater drilling, may be unsuccessful much of the time. Because of the high cost and high risk of exploration, some companies supplement internal development with acquisitions to replace reserves. Alternatively, start-up companies have very high operating costs due to significant investment in projects that often have long lead times before becoming productive.

O&G companies generally have high operating leverage, in which fixed costs (such as exploration and development) account for a relatively high portion of total costs. If revenue declines because of lower sales volume, highly leveraged companies cannot lower total costs as far as less leveraged companies because fixed costs are stationary and do not decrease as sales decrease. As a result, net operating income falls farther for highly leveraged companies. Thus, operating leverage is really a measure of the volatility of the business's earnings in relation to sales. A business with higher operating leverage is riskier than an equivalent business with lower operating leverage. As a result, O&G companies need to closely manage the balance between fixed costs and variable costs. Mineral leases and service contracts often have provisions that make it difficult for a company to stop or slow down development. In the absence of hedging, a commodity price decline during development could cause the project to be unprofitable. While exploration investment can generate significant returns, it may also pose risk if exploration is unsuccessful. Large, long producing fields or basins often generate more predictable cash flow but usually have higher development and operating costs (leases, royalties, etc.).

Royalties and ground lease costs for E&P companies also are significant. Royalty and ground lease rates vary extensively depending on location, when they were acquired, tax rates, and contract structure. A major risk facing O&G companies is overpayment for royalty and ground leases. This risk is especially relevant if the company is a latecomer to a recently discovered field, where the boom mentality on that location pushes up lease rates. Lease overpayment can quickly erode returns, especially if the field does not produce as expected.

Differences Between Oil and Natural Gas

There are key differences between crude oil and natural gas that significantly affect the markets for each. Crude oil, which is typically refined to produce transportation fuels and fuel oils, is a globally traded commodity, and there are many different grades. The most common grades of crude oil are West Texas Intermediate (WTI) and Brent. Both WTI and Brent are classified as "light, sweet" grade crude oils, indicating low density and low sulfur content. This consistency allows oil refineries to convert a higher percentage of the oil into fuel than "heavy, sour" grade crude oils. As a result, sweet crude tends to trade at a premium over heavy crude. Within broad markets, there are submarkets for oil that do not correlate to changes in the broader market, because of the differences in costs to transport the oil to refineries and eventually fuel to the retail market.

Natural gas is primarily used to produce electricity, to heat homes and buildings, and as a base ingredient for industrial products such as plastic, fertilizer, and chemicals. The natural gas market is not directly correlated to oil markets. Natural gas is generally marketed regionally because transport costs are high. Natural gas can be converted to liquid form. Conversion of natural gas to liquefied natural gas (LNG) has increased rapidly in recent years. LNG can be transported over long distances much more easily than natural gas, thus expanding its market. Both the conversion process and specialized transport equipment, however, are costly relative to the amount of energy produced, which diminishes international trade of LNG. Further, there have been legislative proposals to restrict or even prohibit international trade of LNG due to national security concerns.

Types of Oil and Natural Gas Reserves

Reserves are quantities of oil or gas that are expected to be commercially recoverable from known accumulations from a given date forward. All reserve estimates involve some uncertainty. The degree of uncertainty depends on the amount of reliable geologic and engineering data available at the time of estimation, as well as the interpretation of the data. The degree of uncertainty is normally communicated by classifying reserves into two primary categories: proved or unproved. Unproved reserves are far less certain to be recovered than proved reserves and may be classified as probable or possible reserves to reflect the degree of uncertainty in their recoverability. Banks should not rely on unproved reserves as the source of repayment for a loan. The following chart shows the relationship among different types of reserves:

Figure 1: Relationship Among Oil and Gas Reserves

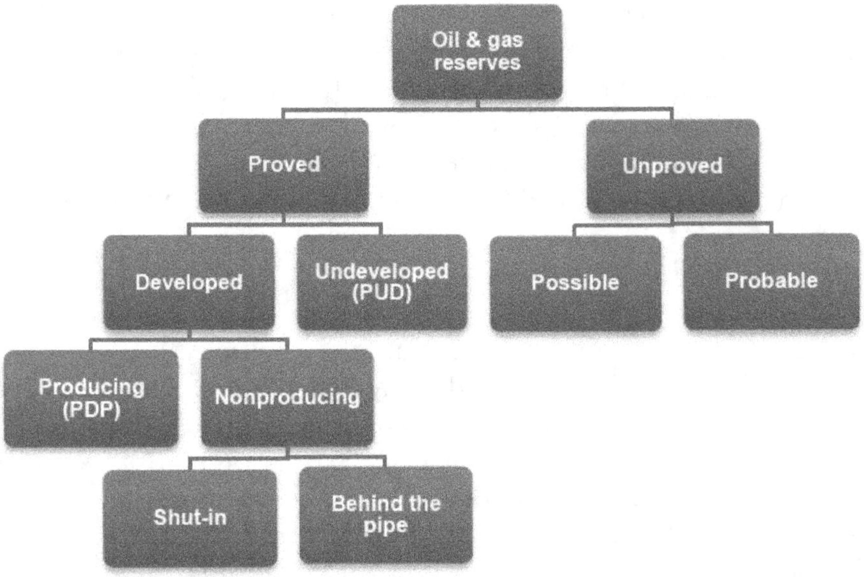

Source: OCC

Proved Reserves

Proved reserves of crude oil and natural gas are estimated quantities that geological and engineering data demonstrate, with reasonable certainty, to be recoverable in future years from known reservoirs using existing economic and operating conditions (i.e., prices and costs as of the date the estimate is made). The O&G industry standard for the probability that reserves will be technically and economically productive is 90 percent. Prices include consideration of changes in existing prices provided by contractual arrangements in the near term and changes based on assumptions about future conditions beyond the near term. Reservoirs are considered proved if economic productive capacity is supported by either actual production or a conclusive formation test. The area of a reservoir considered proved includes

- that portion immediately surrounding any producing well bores.
- the immediately adjoining portions to areas that have not been drilled but can be reasonably judged as economically productive based on available geological and engineering data.
- reserves that can be produced economically through application of improved recovery techniques (such as hydraulic fracturing or other reliable recovery methods). These reserves are included in the "proved" classification when successful testing by an

exploratory project, or the operation of an installed program in the reservoir, provides support for the engineering analysis on which the project or program was based.

Proved reserves can be categorized as developed or undeveloped.

Developed Reserves

Developed O&G reserves are reserves that can be expected to be recovered through existing wells and operating methods. Additional O&G expected to be obtained through the application of fluid injection or other improved recovery techniques for supplementing the natural forces and mechanisms of primary recovery are sometimes included as proved developed reserves. Banks, however, should include these reserves as developed only after either testing via a pilot project or the operation of an installed program confirms (through production response) that increased recovery will be achieved. Developed reserves may be subcategorized as producing or nonproducing.

Producing Reserves

Proved developed reserves subcategorized as producing (PDP) are expected to be recovered from completion intervals that are open and producing at the time of the estimate. Improved recovery reserves are considered producing only after the improved recovery project is in operation. Cash flow generated from the sale of oil or natural gas in the future is the basic premise of reserve-based lending. For this reason, prudence mandates that loan underwriting be predicated primarily on PDP reserves.

Nonproducing Reserves

Proved developed reserves subcategorized as nonproducing (PDNP) include "shut-in" and "behind the pipe" reserves:

- **Proved developed shut-in:** Proved developed properties that are temporarily shut in and not producing due to market conditions or lack of pipeline connections.
- **Proved developed behind the pipe:** Reserves expected to be recovered from zones in existing wells but that will require additional completion work before production starts.

Undeveloped Reserves

Proved undeveloped (PUD) O&G reserves are expected to be recovered from new wells on undrilled acreage, or from existing wells where a relatively major expenditure is required for recompletion. Reserves on undrilled acreage are limited to those drilling units offsetting productive units, where there is reasonable certainty of production once drilled. Proved reserves for other undrilled units can only be claimed when there are demonstrated certainties that the existing productive formation can generate continuity of production. If an application of fluid injection or other improved recovery techniques is contemplated, estimates for PUD reserves should not be attributable to the borrowing base under any circumstances, unless actual tests in the same reservoir and area proved the techniques are effective.

Unproved Reserves

Unproved reserve estimates of crude oil, natural gas, and natural gas liquids are also based on geological and engineering data but do not indicate the high degree of certainty associated with proved reserves.

Probable Reserves

Probable O&G reserves are supported by favorable engineering but are subject to some risk that prevents classification as proved. The O&G industry standard for the probability that reserves will technically and economically produce is 50 percent.

Possible Reserves

Possible reserves are speculative O&G properties where there is a high risk of unsuccessful drilling. The O&G industry standard for the probability that reserves will technically and economically produce is 10 percent.

Banks are expected to monitor the conditions in the markets where they are active and consider them in their monitoring and lending strategies.

Types of Interest in O&G Reserves

O&G lending involves understanding the way the O&G property's interests, reserves, and cash flows are allocated within the capital and ownership structure. Each interest is subject to encumbrance, and the borrower may have numerous entities that hold different interests and have different encumbrances. Conversely, the borrower may subject all interests to a single encumbrance. Properties may be located in various jurisdictions, including different states and countries, but mortgaged under a single loan transaction. The following is a partial list of common types of O&G interests:

- **Mineral interest:** A property interest that is created by an instrument that transfers, by a grant, assignment, reservation, or otherwise, an interest of any kind in coal, O&G, and other minerals.
- **Royalty interest:** A property interest in O&G minerals, whose owner is entitled to a share of production when there is production. A royalty interest is free of the costs of production.
- **Working interest:** A percentage of ownership in an O&G lease that grants its owner the right to explore and produce O&G from a tract of property.
- **Net revenue interest:** A property interest the assignee of a lease actually has in the profits of the mineral-production operations, free of production costs after all overriding royalties are paid out.
- **Overriding royalty interest:** A working interest in the production of O&G rather than a property interest in the minerals in the ground.

O&G Accounting

Accounting approaches often differ significantly among O&G companies. A company may use two methods of accounting for drilling costs: full cost and successful efforts. The choice greatly affects a company's income statement. A full-cost company capitalizes all of its acquisition, exploration, and development costs and does not differentiate between successful and unsuccessful projects. A successful-efforts company only capitalizes costs pertaining to successful projects and acquisitions, amortized over the production life of the projects. If the efforts are unsuccessful, the costs are expensed. The result is that the income statement appears far better for companies that use the full-cost method of accounting for drilling costs.

The reliability of reserve disclosures sometimes varies among companies. Generally, reserve reports that are prepared by an independent, third-party engineer are considered more reliable than internal reports that are audited by third-party engineers. Regardless, O&G companies' annual reserve disclosures can have a material impact on stated earnings. Companies that book reserves liberally may be required to make substantial revisions to their financial statements.

O&G companies that hold derivatives that do not qualify for hedge accounting report their gains and losses on each income statement. Unrealized gains and losses that relate to future production can distort current cash flow analysis and make O&G performance comparisons difficult.

O&G Markets

Bank credit plays an important role in the O&G industry. The highly specialized financing supplied by banks is essential to many O&G exploration and production companies, drilling operators, and service companies.

The traditional role of bank credit in the O&G industry has been to finance E&P activities, including equipment needs, and to provide working capital to service companies. The repayment of O&G production loans depends primarily on the successful gathering and marketing of a commodity, and secondarily on the collateral taken for the loan. In the case of equipment loans and loans to service companies, the ability of the borrower to collect cash payment for contracted services rendered and rental income is typically the primary source of repayment.

Global events and new technologies have had a dramatic effect on O&G price volatility (short-term) and trends (long-term). Volatility comes from shorter-term or one-time incidents such as geopolitical events (e.g., circumstances in the Middle East that threaten to disrupt supply), actual supply disruptions from hurricanes, or sharp recessions in major economies that temporarily reduce demand. Because of this volatility, banks must maintain discipline in their lending practices and follow prudent lending standards as industry fundamentals can change quickly.

Over the long term, rising industrial production and larger automotive fleets in emerging economies support the trend of slowly rising oil prices arising from more demand. Increased production from hydraulic fracturing (known as fracking) in North America and elsewhere is a long-term trend that has increased supply, which somewhat offsets the upward pressure that higher demand places on prices.

Banks continue to be competitive in the O&G credit market. There also are other influential participants, two of which have increased their involvement over time:

- **Equity investors:** Over time, the role of equity investors in the O&G industry has increased significantly as new O&G ownership and financing structures have evolved. These changes have aided banks lending to O&G producers by spreading out credit exposure. The increasingly complex corporate structure of O&G companies also requires that O&G lenders have more specialized expertise and monitoring systems. For example, equity can be structured as a traditional (operating) equity investment in the operating company or a nonoperating investment in an affiliate where the operating company has limited liability exchanged for the capital investment. An example of the latter is a volumetric production payment (VPP) arrangement, an increasingly popular financing structure. Banks need to understand the role that each affiliated entity or sponsor fulfills within the financing structure, and the risks and obligations pertaining to each throughout the various stages of production from exploration, development, production, etc.
- **Bond investors:** Like equity investors, securitization has played an increasingly important role in O&G financing by providing affordable access to capital markets.

O&G Lending Structure

The acquisition and development of O&G reserves are the most common purposes of O&G production lending. These transactions involve financing the location of O&G deposits, the extraction of O&G deposits, and the eventual sale of O&G at a price sufficient to repay the loan.

Structure is especially important in O&G loans. The timing of contractual principal repayments should coincide with the timing of cash flows expected to be received from the project. When principal payments and cash inflows are not properly matched and enforced, the effectiveness of bank management's loan supervision, including the ability to spot performance problems, can be compromised. Poorly structured loans also increase the possibility that proceeds will be used for unintended purposes. Loan structure can affect collateral and other secondary repayment sources, covenant controls, and the quality of loan administration.

Production Loans

The structure of the O&G loan agreement can govern the loan terms and conditions. O&G production loans are typically structured as revolving credit commitments, with terms generally ranging from three to seven years and advances controlled by a borrowing base. The borrowing base is redetermined semiannually, based on an updated engineering evaluation and the bank's current O&G pricing policy (price deck). Discounting the value of nonproducing reserves based on production risks (before applying advance rates) is a common practice. These risk adjustments vary widely by bank and category of reserve.

A production loan can also be structured as a term loan that is reduced by scheduled principal payments. Term facilities are typically used if the loan is made to acquire O&G properties and are the least complicated structure of an O&G production credit. The bank determines the amount it will lend based on engineering reports and makes a one-time advance for the acquisition. Most term loans are amortized with installment principal and interest payments that fully repay the loan over the loan term. Some term loans are structured as "bullet" loans, where the principal balance is paid at maturity.

Another production loan structure is a reducing revolver, which is a combination of a revolver and a term loan. The revolver can increase to a maximum commitment level and then steps down at regular principal payment dates. Regardless of structure, a current engineering report and a corresponding borrowing base are crucial.

Volumetric Production Payment Financing Transactions

Under a VPP financing transaction structure, banks provide financing to an O&G producer and receive a limited overriding royalty interest in the producer's lease of specifically identified reserves. A VPP arrangement is a method to monetize future O&G production. Instead of cash payments, the VPP interest entitles the bank to receive a dedicated share of the hydrocarbons that are produced over a stated term. Additionally, the bank enters into a forward sale agreement to presell the hydrocarbons at a set price (spot price) based on the forward prices for the commodity at the time of the transaction. On the day of settlement, the producer, through the bank, transfers the title to the hydrocarbons to the purchaser of the forward contract. As either an alternative or supplement to selling the forward contract, the bank may mitigate the hydrocarbon price risk using other derivative transactions to hedge the risks, such as commodity swaps. Banks should contact their supervisory offices before engaging in such transactions to ensure the activities can be conducted in a safe and sound manner and in accordance with applicable law. With respect to national banks, please refer to 12 USC 29 and OCC Interpretive Letter 1117 for details on the permissibility of VPP financing transactions.

From the bank's risk perspective, the VPP interest is free and clear of all operating costs, capital expenditures, and taxes. The O&G producer (borrower) retains all of the operational and environmental risks. Commodity price risk is negligible if appropriate hedging techniques are used. The VPP, however, is recourse only to the production from the specified reserve and not the producer's other assets. While the bank has first right to the production up to the specified amount, there is no right to additional production unless the reserves underproduced in a previous period. Therefore, excess production cannot be captured unless there has already been a shortfall. As a result, banks have production risk if the underproduction is permanent or otherwise not replaced by overproduction later.

O&G Equipment Loans

Loans to finance O&G equipment are considered capital debt. The loan should be serviced from business operating cash flow, including any rental income derived from the equipment. Like any equipment loan, the structure should ensure repayment within the useful life of the equipment. These loans have proven to be some of the most troublesome for O&G lenders. The equipment is very expensive, and with a downturn in the industry, much of the equipment sits idle and loses its value as collateral given diminished resale opportunities. There are two major categories of capital loans: drilling rig loans and other equipment.

Borrowers who purchase drilling rigs and O&G service equipment include

- independent drilling contractors and O&G service contractors whose business is to provide drilling and other O&G services to other companies on a contract basis.
- E&P companies that want to own their own drilling rigs. Larger independent companies have access to enough capital to build and operate their own drilling equipment and fracking fleets. This competition has increased pricing pressure on drilling and O&G service companies.

E&P companies assume the drilling risk in a day-rate contract and pay the independent drilling contractor a daily rate to drill the well. The independent driller provides a fixed bid for turnkey contracts and assumes all drilling risks until the well is drilled. Turnkey contracts are typically preferred by operators when drilling risk is high. Consequently, independent drilling contracts provide higher compensation for successful drilling due to the higher risk incurred by the drilling contractor.

A critical factor in evaluating drilling rig loans, particularly for independent contractors, is experience. The drilling contractor must possess sufficient experience, not only to operate the drilling rigs but also to develop industry contacts in order to secure profitable drilling contracts.

Authority and Limits

National banks and federal savings associations are generally permitted to engage in O&G lending by statute. The authority for national banks is found in 12 USC 24(Seventh) while the authority for federal savings associations is found in 12 USC 1464.

A national bank's O&G lending exposure is not specifically limited, provided the volume and nature of the lending does not pose unwarranted risk to the bank's financial condition. Additionally, certain types of O&G lending may require consideration of the requirements of 12 USC 29. (See OCC Interpretive Letter 1117.)

Certain exposure limitations do apply to federal savings associations as set forth in 12 USC 1464(c) and 12 CFR 160.30. O&G loans typically are classified as commercial loans, which cannot exceed 20 percent of total assets, provided that commercial loans in excess of 10 percent of assets must be small business loans.[2] A federal savings association, however, may make O&G loans under other authority, depending on the circumstances.[3] For example, to the extent an O&G loan is secured by nonresidential real property, a federal savings association may make the loan under its nonresidential real property loan authority.[4]

Risks Associated With O&G Production Lending

From a supervisory perspective, risk is the potential that events, expected or unexpected, will have an adverse effect on a bank's earnings, capital, or franchise or enterprise value. The OCC has defined eight categories of risk for bank supervision purposes: credit, interest rate, liquidity, price, operational, compliance, strategic, and reputation. These categories are not mutually exclusive. Any product or service may expose a bank to multiple risks. Risks also may be interdependent and may be positively or negatively correlated. Examiners should be aware of this interdependence and assess the effect in a consistent and inclusive manner. Refer to the "Bank Supervision Process" booklet of the *Comptroller's Handbook* for an expanded discussion of banking risks and their definitions.

The risks associated with O&G lending are credit, interest rate, liquidity, operational, compliance, strategic, and reputation.

Credit Risk

Banks that finance O&G exploration, development, and production assume the risk associated with the borrower's ability to successfully find O&G resources, extract them from the ground, and deliver them to the midstream market for a profit. An O&G company's repayment capacity is vulnerable to weather conditions, commodity price volatility, changing government regulations, geopolitical events, and infrastructure or labor market shortages, none of which may be under the borrower's control. Borrowers can mitigate many of these risks by using diversification strategies (both geographic and product mix), purchasing insurance, integrating operations, using hedging and structured financing techniques, and investing in ownership of service companies or equipment.

Market Volatility

Volatile market prices for O&G present the primary repayment risk for the O&G borrower. Large price fluctuations can occur because of weather, supply and demand, and geopolitical

---

[2] 12 USC 1464(c)(2)(A). Small business loans include any loan to a small business (defined in 13 CFR 121) and any loan that does not exceed $2 million and is for commercial, corporate, business, or agricultural purposes. See the definitions of "Small business loans and loans to small businesses" and "Small business" in 12 CFR 160.3.

[3] 12 CFR 160.31(a) provides that if a loan is authorized under more than one section of the Home Owners' Loan Act, a federal savings association may designate under which section the loan has been made. Such a loan may be apportioned among appropriate categories.

[4] 12 USC 1464(c)(2)(B). This statute generally limits nonresidential real property loans to 400 percent of the federal savings association's capital.

events. Because crude oil is typically traded in U.S. dollars, changes in the value of the dollar also may affect oil prices. Producers have the ability to hedge their production to alleviate large price variations, and banks often require such price protection by using commodity derivative products. Hedges, however, tend to be short term and may be costly if the commodity price is already depressed. Commodity swaps, call options, put options, futures contracts, and forward contracts are the most common derivatives used. Call options (ceilings) and put options (floors) can be arranged to form collars. Some collars, known as participating collars, have provisions that allow the producer to participate in a portion of the upside (i.e., when the market price moves above the ceiling). Others may have disappearing ceilings, known as knockouts. A producer also may choose a simple swap, which usually means that the borrower is swapping a floating market price for a fixed price. E&P companies use future and forward contracts to lock in O&G at a future sell price. The bank's written O&G lending policy should address the use of commodity derivatives. The policy should include a discussion of counterparty risk, operational risk, the percentage of a borrower's PDP reserves that should be hedged, and the maximum tenor of hedges.

Government Policies and Legal Risks

O&G production is highly regulated in the United States, and changes in governmental policies can have a dramatic effect on the industry. Regulations may differ among states or even counties. Private landowners often own mineral rights in the United States, but public entities often own mineral rights abroad, causing ownership, environmental liability, and business risks to vary depending on where the operation is located.

O&G companies need large areas of land to develop and operate wells. O&G production can cause significant pollution, and there is extensive state and federal regulation of access and environmental remediation. Additionally, government restrictions can affect the type of drilling technology used to extract O&G. Technologies new to mass commercialization, such as fracking, are particularly susceptible to regulatory restrictions. In such cases, technology is rapidly adopted by the industry, but health, safety, and environmental regulations are finalized after a significant time lag. If the regulation involves production restraints or even cessation, banks that have made loans based on the technology and communities that have built up around the technology will be significantly harmed. Examples of regulation-induced production restraints include restriction by certain states on fracking and restrictions on drilling in Alaska and the Gulf of Mexico. Government regulation might also unexpectedly increase production costs through mandates to remove equipment when pumping is finished, mandates on the use of alternative fuel, and foreign government policies in O&G producing countries. O&G companies also face compliance (legal liability) and reputation risks due to accidents, such as explosions or oil spills that can injure or kill workers, damage property, or cause environmental contamination. Such events can result in significant strain on an O&G borrower's repayment capacity if insurance coverage is inadequate.

Limited Purpose Collateral

O&G-related collateral may have few or no alternative uses to support values when loan repayment problems arise. For production loans, there is usually a secondary market whereby, at a price, production rights can be sold. In the case of O&G equipment, auction companies can dispose of bank collateral on an as-needed basis. Demand for specialized O&G equipment, however, closely correlates with O&G commodity prices. As a result, when O&G prices fall, equipment values often fall as well. Additionally, during periods of severe price declines, banks may have difficulty liquidating equipment at a reasonable price.

Interest Rate Risk

The level of interest rate risk attributed to the bank's O&G lending activities depends on the composition of the bank's loan portfolio and the degree to which the underwriting terms of its loans, such as tenor and pricing, expose the bank's revenue to changes in interest rates. Most O&G production financing provided by banks is on a floating rate basis, which makes the interest rate sensitivity for the lending bank relatively low. Banks that provide fixed-rate financing for extended terms expose themselves to interest rate risk to the extent that shorter-term liabilities or structured wholesale borrowings fund these loans.

Liquidity Risk

The nature of O&G lending can result in higher liquidity risk at some banks, especially smaller banks in areas where changes in O&G supply and demand strongly affect the economy. High levels of correlated credit concentrations may be common under those circumstances, and a bank's liquidity can become strained if unfavorable market conditions result in borrowers having difficulty making loan payments or in reduced public and private deposits. Longer-term liquidity pressure may arise at some banks because of capped or abandoned wells, reduced exploration, and population migration due to high local unemployment. A bank's inability to liquidate or sell O&G loans at a reasonable price during sustained downturns in the O&G market also may cause liquidity risk.

Operational Risk

O&G lending carries an elevated level of operational risk due to the complexity of the industry and O&G borrowers as well as the corresponding need to maintain effective monitoring and control systems. A lack of understanding of operational risks, or failure to monitor and control them, may lead to serious credit weaknesses, including ultimate collection problems. O&G operational risks are affected by

- complex financing structures often used in the O&G industry.
- volatile commodity markets that must be routinely monitored.
- reliance on complex engineering reports and inspections to monitor the borrowing base, reserve value, production levels, and depletion.
- different legal requirements across jurisdictions.
- complex corporate and capital structures that may change over time.
- routine use of hedging techniques and financial derivatives that must be documented and understood.
- environmental and safety hazards that must be monitored and evaluated.

Compliance Risk

O&G lending is subject to the same regulatory and compliance issues as other types of commercial lending. Given the numerous restrictions governing O&G exploration and production, O&G lending can be vulnerable to specific types of compliance risk, such as potential environmental liability should the bank repossess contaminated collateral. There are also banking regulations discussed in this booklet that govern an institution's risk management.

Strategic Risk

A sound O&G lending program necessarily includes management and staffs that have the knowledge and experience required to recognize, assess, mitigate, and monitor the risks that are unique to O&G. Prudent O&G lending requires specialized expertise. Failure to invest in sufficient staff and infrastructure, or provide effective oversight of O&G lending, can significantly increase the bank's strategic risk profile while also affecting other interrelated risks such as credit and reputation.

Reputation Risk

Lending to companies that the public perceives to be negligent in preventing environmental damage, hazardous accidents, or weak fiduciary management can damage a bank's reputation. A bank also puts its reputation at risk if it reduces the availability of credit to small businesses dependent on the O&G industry, even when these decisions are prudent.

Some O&G transactions are syndicated throughout the institutional market because of their size and risk characteristics. A bank's failure to meet its legal or fiduciary responsibilities in sourcing and syndicating O&G loans can damage its reputation and impair its ability to compete successfully in this line of business.

As previously discussed, some O&G loans are only a part of complex structured finance arrangements. These arrangements typically involve the structuring of cash flows and the allocation of risk among borrowers and investors to meet specific customer objectives more efficiently. The transactions often involve professionals with specialized expertise and may involve creation of special purpose entities. Although the majority of transactions serve legitimate business purposes, banks may be exposed to significant reputation and legal (compliance) risks if they enter into transactions without appropriate due diligence, oversight, and internal controls. Further guidance pertaining to structured finance is contained in OCC Bulletin 2007-1, "Complex Structured Finance Transactions: Notice of Final Interagency Statement."

Risk Management

The OCC expects each bank to identify, measure, monitor, and control risk by implementing an effective risk management system appropriate for its size and the complexity of its operations. When examiners assess the effectiveness of a bank's risk management system, they consider the bank's policies, processes, personnel, and control systems. Refer to the "Bank Supervision Process" and "Loan Portfolio Management" booklets of the *Comptroller's Handbook* for an expanded discussion of risk management.

Loan Policy and Governance

A bank's O&G production loan policy should include[5]

- O&G lending objectives and risk appetite, including acceptable types of O&G loans, portfolio distribution (concentrations of credit), lending market or territory, and risk limits measured as a percentage of capital.
- a comprehensive, written O&G engineering policy that provides specific guidelines for preparing engineering reports.
- requirements for the structure, reporting lines, and oversight of the O&G lending department and engineering department.
- underwriting standards and approval requirements that are specific to lending to the O&G industry, including measurement of O&G reserves and production history, financial analysis expectations, advance and discount rates on various reserve types, pricing parameters, covenant and structure expectations, approval authority, and policy exception authority.

Additionally, policies should address O&G credit administration and loan documentation standards pertinent to O&G lending, including

- reserve production and depletion.
- new project development.
- reserve replacement.
- borrowing base redetermination.
- stress testing.
- collateral re-valuation.
- collateral documentation and title verification.

The bank's board of directors is responsible for ensuring control systems are in place to monitor compliance with established O&G lending policies. The results should be an important consideration in a bank's allowance for loan and lease losses (ALLL) and capital and liquidity planning processes and should be taken into consideration as part of the board's action to approve risk limits as a percentage of total capital pertaining to O&G lending. The board should update and approve O&G policies annually.

---

[5] As discussed in the "Overview" section, this booklet addresses only the more specialized E&P segment of the O&G industry. Due to the variety of companies engaged in E&P, the booklet includes some discussion of equipment lending and other considerations that may be applicable to midstream or upstream companies. The scope of the "Risk Management" and "Examination Procedures" sections is limited to lending to the E&P segment of the industry.

Bank management should provide the board of directors with an analysis of the risk posed by O&G lending activities as well as risks correlated to the O&G industry and their potential effect on the bank's asset quality, earnings, capital, and liquidity. Management should consider the potential impact on earnings and capital and on the bank's operating strategy of O&G lending under stressed market conditions and economic downturns, as well as normal market conditions. The OCC expects the board of directors to ensure that the bank maintains adequate capital relative to concentration risks, including concentrations pertaining to O&G-related lending. Refer to the "Concentrations of Credit" booklet of the *Comptroller's Handbook* for more details pertaining to concentration risk. There also may be cases in which the potential risk to capital is so severe that reduction of the concentration or suspension of O&G loan originations will be the most effective risk mitigation action.

Staffing

O&G production lending involves unique, and sometimes complex, risks that require specialized knowledge and controls. The O&G lending staff should possess sufficient technical expertise for the volume and complexity of O&G lending that will be performed and monitored. Given that O&G lending decisions rely on quality engineering reports, the technical expertise of the engineering staff is critical. The board should ensure that the size of the engineering staff is sufficient to enable timely completion of work so all borrowing base redeterminations can be promptly completed. The depth within the engineering staff should enable succession and continuation of quality work during times of change or adversity. Additionally, sufficient resources should be allocated to staff development and continuing education.

The board should ensure that the O&G engineering function is independent of the O&G loan production and credit approval functions. While engineers may have communication with and input from loan production personnel to facilitate credit analysis, the reporting line for the engineering function should be separate from the production line. Engineer performance evaluations or approved lists, when using third-party engineers, should be performed by someone who does not have credit approval authority. The engineering department may have input into credit decisions, for example, veto power, but should not have loan approval authority. The compensation program for engineers should not include incentives for O&G loan volume generated by the lending department.

Underwriting

Prudent O&G loan underwriting shares many of the same characteristics as lending to commercial enterprises in other industries. A bank's O&G underwriting criteria should consider the borrower's experience and track record in managing similar operations or projects. The underwriting process begins with current, accurate, and complete credit data. The bank should obtain fiscal balance sheets and operating statements (financial statements) from the borrower each year. It is also a prudent practice to obtain and analyze interim financial statements. Specific requirements for credit information should be detailed in the bank's loan policy.

O&G lenders should analyze certain factors that are particularly important to underwriting O&G credits. An effective set of written guidelines should govern the underwriting process and subsequent loan administration.

At a minimum, the guidelines should require

- thorough evaluation of the borrower's character and history of managing debt repayment.
- in-depth financial analysis of the borrower and any guarantors.
- reliable collateral evaluations, including current independent engineering reports for O&G production loans, and margins or other steps to minimize credit risk.
- risk adjusting the discount value of nonproducing reserves before applying advance rates.
- structuring loans in accordance with the type of borrowing and the expected source of repayment.
- maximum advance rates for each category of O&G reserve.
- maximum loan term.
- minimum levels of property and liability insurance.
- minimum limits on the number of producing wells.
- acceptable status with state specific governing authority.
- effective ongoing financial and maintenance covenants, including semiannual redetermination of borrowing bases for O&G production loans and more frequent on-site inspections (field visits) during periods of high volatility or risk in O&G markets.
- restructuring expectations should the borrowing base decline below the outstanding balance. (Typically, banks restructure reducing revolving lines to fully amortize no later than 120 percent of the half-life or 60 percent of the economic life of the reserves.)
- an assessment of the impact of hedging and when hedging will be required.
- ongoing monitoring of O&G development, production, and the borrowing base.

Establishing the Borrowing Base

The borrowing base for O&G loans is the estimated value of O&G that can be produced from the mineral rights. It is determined by analyzing prior production reports and independent engineering valuations.

The borrowing base formula, as established in the loan agreement, should govern the maximum amount of revolving O&G credit available at any one time. The revolving credit is generally secured by O&G reserves, which are working assets, i.e., assets that are used over time to repay the loan. Ideally, there should be diversification in the geographical location of fields or reservoirs where the reserves are situated. At a minimum, banks should set limits on the lowest number of producing wells (i.e., production concentration) needed to establish an acceptable borrowing base. The value of the reserves helps determine the loan amount and dictates the availability of funds. Typically, a borrower can draw against the credit as many times and as often as needed up to the lesser of the available borrowing base or the note amount. The outstanding balance of the loan should fluctuate with the cash needs of the borrower, subject to the availability constraints of the borrowing base. Credit availability is restored when principal is repaid from the conversion of assets to cash and collateral is restored to the borrowing base.

Ideally, the borrowing base will be based primarily on PDP properties. These properties should be producing satisfactorily for a period—typically six months or more—that is sufficient to generate reliable production results (run data). The proceeds of this production should be sufficient to amortize the debt over a reasonable amount of time (three to seven years) with some portion of reserves remaining. Maximum advance rates vary by bank for PDP reserves (typically ranging from 50 percent to 65 percent of the present worth of future net income [PWFNI]), with much lower advance rates for PDNP reserves, such as shut-in and behind the pipe, and PUD reserves.

When banks advance on PDNP or PUD reserves, it is particularly important to fully support the risk factors used to determine the discount rate. Banks should not advance on unproved reserves. Some banks' advance rates are based on total risk-adjusted proved reserves, including PDP, PDNP, and PUD reserves. In these cases, maximum advance rates vary by bank (generally ranging from 50 percent to 65 percent of the total risk-adjusted PWFNI of these reserves). Regardless of a bank's advance rates on the various categories of reserves, banks should establish a limit for the contribution that reserves other than PDP contribute to the borrowing base. There should be limits on the contribution any one well can make to the borrowing base.

Financial Analysis

Prudent O&G loan underwriting requires that O&G lenders have a thorough understanding of the borrower's operating environment and future cash flow capability. Because an O&G company's cash flow is vulnerable to a wide range of risks, O&G lenders need to have a complete understanding of the company's cash flow sensitivity and balance sheet.

Sensitivity analysis in the underwriting process should estimate the impact that sustained changes in market conditions would have on a company's repayment ability. As part of the underwriting process, banks often prepare base case and sensitivity case analyses on the ability of the conversion of the underlying collateral into cash to repay the loan. A base case analysis uses standard assumption scenarios. A conservative base case approach is to discount current prices against the forward curve. A sensitivity case analysis subjects the O&G reserves to adverse external factors such as lower market prices or higher operating expenses to ascertain the effect on loan repayment.

Reserves are a significant, if not the most significant, asset on an O&G company's balance sheet. The reserves are subject to both price volatility and depletion. As a result, O&G companies are typically more dependent on their balance sheet than companies in most other industries. O&G lenders need to analyze and assess a borrower's balance sheet to understand how the company's financial condition would be affected by changes in the operating environment and market conditions. An O&G borrower's operating leverage position, liquidity, and access to capital are often critical to the company's ability to withstand adverse conditions.

The analysis should also consider any necessary adjustments pertaining to accounting, nonrecurring gains and losses, acquisitions or company restructure, and hedging, all of which are common in the industry at certain stages of the O&G business cycle. O&G companies capitalize exploration and development costs in different ways depending on the accounting method selected. Because these costs are often significant, leverage measures (e.g., earnings before interest, taxes, depreciation, and amortization) that do not include expense capitalization may reflect a stronger position than is likely for some O&G companies. Additionally, the O&G business is highly capital intensive due to the need for almost constant reserve replacement. As a result, liquidity analysis should consider the amount of cash such projects are likely to use.

As with other types of lending, when a bank relies on a guaranty to support approval of the loan, a guarantor global financial condition (GFC) analysis should be performed during the initial underwriting and approval stage. The guarantor(s) must be financially responsible, meaning the guarantor must have the capacity and willingness to support the loan. Determination of capacity should include a current and comprehensive analysis of the guarantor's GFC, including legal structure, asset valuations, liquidity, sources and amounts of recurring cash flow, actual and contingent liabilities, and any other relevant factors necessary to demonstrate capacity to support the loan. This analysis should consider the total number and amount of guarantees currently extended by a guarantor and the effect such guarantees have on the guarantor's cash flow. A global cash flow analysis should always be part of the GFC analysis. Subsequent to loan approval and funding, a periodic financial analysis of a guarantor is appropriate and prudent for most lending relationships. If the guarantor's financial condition is complex or evidences significant risk, a periodic guarantor GFC analysis should be performed to monitor other projects and the guarantor's financial capacity.

Collateral Valuation

Engineering Function

A critical step in assessing the credit and collateral of O&G production loans is the engineering function analysis. Cash flow generated from the future sale of encumbered oil or gas reserves is the intended, and in most cases the primary, source of repayment. Reserve interests are typically the most significant asset held by an O&G company and the most significant, if not the only, asset pledged as collateral. Therefore, the integrity of engineering data that depict value of the future cash flow stream is critical to the initial lending decision and equally important to an examiner in the assessment of the credit quality.

Estimating O&G reserves is difficult and not always precise. The reliability of reserve estimates can be inconsistent depending on the assumptions used by engineers. Because O&G prices and production are subject to significant risks that cannot be predicted or controlled, reserve development and extraction operations are sometimes delayed, suspended, or even stopped.

Acceptable engineering reports should be independent, detailed analyses of the O&G reserves that are prepared by a competent engineer. Reports are sometimes prepared by an engineer hired by the borrower. These reports should be thoroughly evaluated by the bank's internal engineering department or an external engineer hired by the bank, to ensure the reserves are valued properly.[6] The bank's internal engineering department should not participate in the credit approval process, except to veto proposed loans if authorized by the board. The engineering report should address four critical concerns:

- **Pricing:** O&G prices must be realistic and fully supported. Banks and independent engineers typically use a price deck to determine the assumed future price of O&G production. The price deck is used in calculations, modeling, predictions, underwriting, and ongoing monitoring. Price decks should be updated at least semiannually and based on average prices over time using possible ranges for price variation. The engineering report should indicate consideration for both price deflation and cost inflation over the lives of the properties.

- **Costs:** Cost assumptions must also be realistic and fully supported. Costs affect the economic life of reserves in three ways: exploration costs, development costs, and production costs. Production costs are typically a key focus in underwriting because the borrowing base is based primarily on PDP reserves. If further exploration or development is planned, however, engineering reports may include exploration and development costs. Production costs include operating and maintenance expenditures for materials, supplies, fuel, property and severance taxes, insurance, maintenance and repairs, etc. Development costs may include roads, utilities, drilling pads, site facilities, development wells, wellheads, well casing, and pipe and well equipment. Exploration costs include testing and surveying O&G prospects outside of known productive fields, areas, or reservoirs. Regardless of the accounting method used by the borrower, engineering reports should include significant costs to estimate reserve value.

- **Discount rate:** The discount rate depends on current market factors that consider the possibility that future cash flows will not be paid as expected. Assumptions used to determine the discount rate should be fully supported.

- **Timing:** The engineering report should be no more than six months old and under no circumstances more than 12 months old. Recent significant price fluctuations or changes in interest rates may require bank management to adjust the valuation of the reserves to reflect current conditions.

In those cases where the engineering reports do not meet one or more of the above criteria, the examiner may need to use other methods, e.g., recent cash flow histories, to determine the current collateral value. In addition, appropriate comments should be included in the report of examination and recommendations made to bank management for improving its engineering reporting and requirements.

Equipment

Many O&G equipment loans that are approved for acquisition or development are made separate from O&G production loans because some or all of the equipment will not remain at the drilling site. In some cases, the equipment and working capital loans are combined.

---

[6] For further guidance pertaining to the use of third parties, please refer to "Third-Party Relationships: Risk Management Guidance," OCC bulletin 2013-29, October 30, 2013.

Banks also sometimes cross-collateralize and cross-default loans to one borrower across multiple loans. Due to the limited use of some O&G equipment, banks may attempt to sell the business as a whole rather than repossess limited use collateral when an O&G company is under financial duress.

The bank should document drilling rigs and other O&G equipment used as collateral. Depending on the type of equipment, especially if it is specialized or costly to relocate, the bank should obtain independent appraisals by firms with specialized expertise. If an updated collateral valuation results in new values, these values should be reflected on the borrower's financial statements. If the equipment is working under a high utilization rate, repair costs and accelerated depreciation should be considered in the valuation. Developing technologies can cause some O&G equipment to become obsolete or require substantial investment to retrofit. Government regulations can also affect the O&G technology that is used. Banks should understand the impact of new O&G technologies and consider the effects on their equipment valuation when it is appropriate.

Credit Administration

Ongoing Monitoring

Ongoing monitoring is critically important to prudent O&G lending. It requires not only remaining abreast of the borrower's operations but also independently keeping up with market events that may affect the borrower. Price decks should be updated at least semiannually. Banks should regularly monitor O&G production output and compare it to assumptions provided in the engineering report. When there is significant deviation, a new or updated engineering analysis should be considered. Banks should assess current market prices and the discount rate in comparison with prior assumptions. The updated lender analysis should be documented and consider whether the borrower's ability to amortize debt has deteriorated to a point below the bank's underwriting standards.

The quality of financial information and subsequent analysis is an integral part of any O&G credit. This analysis should include

- determining the adequacy and monitoring of operating cash flow to service debt.
- determining compliance with any financial covenants, including borrowing base limitations, contained in the loan agreement.
- reviewing the reasonableness of budget assumptions and projections.
- comparing projections with actual results.
- assessing working capital adequacy.
- analyzing net worth and leverage changes.
- assessing the impact of capital expenses and acquisitions.

Sensitivity analysis in the underwriting process should estimate the impact of changes to the borrower's primary and secondary repayment ability. Updates to both the base case and sensitivity case analyses should be performed at least annually. As in the underwriting sensitivity analysis, loan repayment should fall within the standards set by the bank's policy.

Collateral Documentation

O&G lending has unique requirements for documentation and perfection of security interests in collateral. The ownership of O&G is assigned as real property while it is still in the ground but changes to personal property when it is extracted from the well. Below is a short synopsis of the documentation requirements:

- **Deed of trust or real estate mortgage:** The deed of trust or real estate mortgage (depending on the state in which the property is located) should provide for the assignment of O&G proceeds, which allows the bank to request that payments from the reserve purchaser be distributed directly to the bank. A bank may or may not perfect its assignment of the lease proceeds, but this clause in the document is necessary if the bank ever desires to do so.
- **Title opinions:** A title opinion should be obtained on loans secured primarily by O&G reserves. This opinion should be prepared by a competent O&G attorney and approved by bank counsel or the board of directors. This is especially important when there is a collateral concentration, a new borrower, or properties that are new to the borrower.
- **UCC-1:** A UCC-1 form should be filed to perfect the bank's security interest in all equipment on the lease as well as the proceeds from the lease. A UCC filing should also be required when the operator of the lease is a significant working interest owner. A UCC filing must be recorded with the Secretary of State and in the county (or parish if in Louisiana) where the O&G gas lease is located.
- **Lien search:** A lien search should be performed before funding and documented in the file to determine the existence of any prior liens. This is normally completed in conjunction with the title opinion. In the rare case that a title opinion is not obtained, a lien search should be done as a minimum precaution.
- **Transfer or division orders:** Copies of transfer or division orders should be obtained from the reserve purchaser. Transfer/division orders usually are not available until at least 60 days after a loan is made if the loan is for the acquisition of such property. Most title opinions verify existence of proper payee on division orders to assist in the determination of ownership (division order title opinion) when title is being transferred from a seller to the buyer. New division orders are issued to the new owner from a certified copy of a filed assignment or deed of trust.
- **Appraisal/valuation:** Documentation of the value of the O&G-related collateral should be an integral part of the file. Whether the loan is for equipment or O&G production, a valuation of that collateral is necessary.
- **Leases and operating agreements:** If applicable, the file should contain copies of all agreements that the debtor has entered into with others that involve the O&G property that is pledged as collateral.
- **Equipment lists and valuation:** If possible, a complete listing of all equipment found on an O&G lease, including models and serial numbers, should be in the file. Since many leases contain hundreds of wells, however, it may not be practical to obtain such information. At a minimum, collateral needed to support term debt should be inspected and valued on a periodic basis. Collateral condition and marketability assessments should be included in the documentation.

- **Conveyance documents:** All conveyance documents related to an O&G transaction should be obtained, particularly when a title opinion is not obtained or the bank is financing the purchase of the producing collateral. Normal conveyance documents would include assignments as well as purchase agreements.
- **Certificate of insurance:** Documentation showing that insurance premiums are paid up to date and that collateral is appropriately covered against potential perils should be obtained.
- **Phase I environmental report:** This document should be required for acquisition financing.

Exception Monitoring

Similar to other types of lending, banks should have a system to monitor O&G loans that are more liberal than the lending policy or practices would normally permit. The bank should have a process to identify, approve, document, and monitor the loan policy and underwriting exceptions. Additionally, banks should track exceptions on an ongoing basis. To gain the maximum benefit from such a process, bank management information systems (MIS) should provide data, not only on individual exceptions but also on the aggregate level. Such aggregated data can provide a more complete picture of risk in the portfolio and reveal weaknesses in the underwriting process, or in the policy itself, that may need to be addressed.

Concentrations

Excessive O&G loan concentrations have been a key factor in the failure of some banks during periods of steep price declines. Banks with regional concentrations in areas that are heavily dependent on the O&G economy can be severely affected beyond the direct lending for O&G production. For example, during periods of either slowing demand or oversupply, O&G companies can slow drilling and exploration or even shut down unprofitable wells. Ancillary O&G businesses, such as O&G service companies, water haulers, and O&G construction companies, either lay off employees or move operations to a more profitable area. Banks that finance local hotels, housing projects, restaurants, convenience stores, etc., in the area are likely to have correlated sensitivity to the O&G industry. Bank management may also face other correlated risks due to funding concentrations, deposit declines during periods of significant local unemployment, or local municipality financial problems (e.g., bond defaults and public deposit reductions). Because of correlations among O&G-related risk factors, stress testing can be an important part of a bank's risk management process. Further guidance is contained in the "Concentrations of Credit" booklet of the *Comptroller's Handbook*.

Environmental Issues

As previously discussed, there are significant environmental risks that can affect O&G borrowers. Some examples of environmental issues, such as large oil spills and debates on the safety of fracturing techniques, have been widely publicized in recent years. Environmental problems can cause project delays, terminate drilling, increase costs, impair cash flow, and reduce collateral values. In some instances, environmental problems can cause significant losses. If banks become responsible for repossessed property, they can be held financially accountable for environmental remediation under provisions of the Comprehensive Environmental Response, Compensation, and Liability Act. Significant environmental disasters also can severely increase reputation risks for responsible parties. As a result, potential liabilities can greatly exceed the amount of the original loan. Banks should perform appropriate due diligence, including independent environmental engineering reports when appropriate, to understand any existing environmental issues and potential environmental risks. Both the borrower's operations and the collateral should be considered in this analysis.

Allowance for Loan and Lease Losses

Banks should segment O&G loans in their ALLL analyses when there is a concentration due to the unique risks that affect borrower performance. Banks also should consider the extent of exposure to oil production versus natural gas, risk within particular geographies, and other risk factors to determine if further segmentation is necessary. When changes or other significant events pose additional risks, banks should consider adjusting their historical loss rates to ensure that the ALLL is adequately funded. Further guidance is contained in the "Allowance for Loan and Lease Losses" booklet of the *Comptroller's Handbook*.

Credit Risk Rating Considerations

As with other types of loans, O&G loans adequately protected by the current sound worth and debt service capacity of the borrower, guarantor, or underlying collateral generally should not be classified for supervisory purposes. Similarly, loans to sound borrowers that are refinanced or renewed in accordance with prudent underwriting standards should not be classified unless well-defined weaknesses that jeopardize repayment exist. A bank should not be criticized for continuing to carry loans with weaknesses that resulted in classification or special mention rating as long as the bank has a well-conceived and effective workout plan for such borrowers, and effective internal controls to manage the level of these loans.

When evaluating O&G loans for possible classification or a "special mention" rating, examiners should apply the uniform rating definitions found in the "Rating Credit Risk" booklet of the *Comptroller's Handbook*. To determine the appropriate classification, examiners should consider all information relevant to evaluating the prospects that the loan will be repaid. This information includes the borrower's creditworthiness; the value of and cash flow provided by the borrower's operation and all collateral supporting the loan; and any support provided by financially responsible guarantors and co-borrowers.

When risk rating O&G facilities, it is important to keep in mind that O&G lending is a borrowing-base, collateral-focused type of commercial lending. The initial step to assessing the creditworthiness of O&G loans is an analysis of the engineering function. The integrity and reliability of the engineering data are critical in determining the appropriate risk rating because these data are used to predict future cash flow, which is usually the primary source of repayment.

In those cases where the engineering reports do not meet one or more of the criteria listed in the "Risk Management" section of this booklet, the examiner may need to use other methods, e.g., recent cash flow histories, to determine the current collateral value and appropriately risk rate the facility. Examiners should also analyze any pricing assumptions that are not adequately documented and supported.

Examiners must consider the quality of the underlying collateral, which should primarily be valued on PDP properties. If any of the following circumstances are present, examiners must perform a comprehensive analysis of the credit to determine if the loan has potential or well-defined weaknesses:

- The loan balance exceeds 65 percent of the discounted PWFNI of PDP, or the cash flow analysis indicates that the loan will not amortize over four to five years.
- The credit is not performing in accordance with terms such as repayment of interest and principal.
- Advance rates exceed the bank's limits or industry standards for reserves other than PDP.
- Frequent over-advances.
- Excessive operating leverage.
- Significant current or likely future disruptions in production.
- Frequent financial statement revisions or any changes in chosen accounting method.
- Maintenance or capital expenditures significantly exceed budgeted forecasts.
- The credit is identified by the bank as a "problem" credit.

If, after performing the analysis, the examiner determines that the borrower's circumstances represent well-defined weaknesses, the loan is troubled and classification is warranted. The examiner must evaluate the quality of the underlying collateral and collateral trends. The entire outstanding balance of an E&P loan does not necessarily warrant classification, especially if there is sufficient cash flow to service all or part of the loan it is dedicated to (e.g., PDP reserves pledged to it). There is no substitute for a specific, individual analysis of the applicable credit and collateral factors pertaining to the loan. Accepted guidelines should be flexibly applied and should not replace examiner judgment. The following guidelines are used for classifying a troubled O&G loan:

- When debt repayment depends on the underlying collateral and there are no other available and reliable sources of repayment,
  - the portion of the loan balance that is secured by up to 65 percent of discounted PWFNI should be classified no worse than "substandard." A lesser percentage or less severe criticism may be appropriate in cases where a reliable means of repayment exists for a portion of the debt. The 65 percent measure should be used when the discounted PWFNI is determined using historical production data (decline curve analysis engineering). When less than 75 percent of the reserve estimate is determined using historical production data, or the discounted PWFNI is predicated on engineering estimates of the volume of O&G flow (volumetric or analogy based engineering data) the collateral value assigned to substandard should be reduced accordingly.

- the remaining balance, but not more than 100 percent of discounted PWFNI of PDP, should be classified "doubtful" when the potential for full loss may be mitigated by the outcome of certain pending events, or when loss is expected but the amount of the loss cannot be reasonably determined.
- the portion of the loan balance that exceeds the value of the collateral, and is clearly uncollectible, should be classified "loss."
- For equipment loans, a current independent appraisal of the equipment should establish the collateral value.

Ideally, the borrowing base will be based primarily on PDP properties. In addition to PDP, however, E&P credits may include other proved reserves such as PDNP, shut-in, behind the pipe, and PUD. Due to the wide range of variables that affect the productivity of these other proved reserves, there are not widely accepted collateral margin guidelines or methods to determine risk ratings for funds advanced against these reserves. While the acceptable margin levels vary by bank or even by borrower, only in unusual circumstances should examiners discount other proved reserves within ranges as soft as PDP discounts. Under no circumstances should unproved reserves be considered in the collateral valuation analysis.

Examiners must determine the current status of each property, estimate an appropriate value of the expected reserves, and apply a discount based on the production risk associated with that property. For example, property that is shut in due to a shortage of pipeline or other transportation to market presents different risk characteristics than a property that is shut in due to lingering price pressures affecting the commodity.

Examination Procedures

This booklet contains expanded procedures for examining specialized activities or specific products or services that warrant extra attention beyond the core assessment contained in the "Community Bank Supervision," "Large Bank Supervision," and "Federal Branches and Agencies Supervision" booklets of the *Comptroller's Handbook*. Examiners determine which expanded procedures to use, if any, during examination planning or after drawing preliminary conclusions during the core assessment.

Scope

These procedures are designed to help examiners tailor the examination to each bank and determine the scope of the O&G production lending examination. This determination should consider work performed by internal and external auditors and other independent risk control functions and by other examiners on related areas. Examiners need to perform only those objectives and steps that are relevant to the scope of the examination as determined by the following objective. Seldom will every objective or step of the expanded procedures be necessary.

Objective: To determine the scope of the examination of O&G production lending and identify examination objectives and activities necessary to meet the needs of the supervisory strategy for the bank.

1. Review the following sources of information and note any previously identified problems related to O&G lending that require follow-up:

    - Supervisory strategy
    - Examiner-in-charge's (EIC) scope memorandum
    - OCC's information system
    - Previous reports of examination and work papers
    - Internal and external audit reports and work papers
    - Bank management's responses to previous reports of examination and audit reports
    - Bank correspondence pertaining to O&G lending
    - Customer complaints and litigation

2. Obtain the results of such reports as the Uniform Bank Performance Reports and Canary. Identify any concerns, trends, or changes involving O&G lending since the last examination. Examiners should be alert to growth rates, changes in portfolio composition, loan yields, and other factors that may affect credit risk.

3. Obtain and review policies, procedures, and reports that bank management uses to supervise O&G lending, including internal risk assessments. Consider

    - portfolio strategies, risk limits, and risk management guidelines.
    - loan trial balance, past due accounts, and loans in nonaccrual status.

- loan commitment and pipeline reports showing commitments and undisbursed funds.
- internal loan review reports.
- credit risk rating reports, including a list of "watch" credits.
- problem loan reports for adversely rated O&G loans.
- concentration reports and board-approved concentration limits.
- loan policy exception report.
- financial statement and collateral exception reports.
- financial statement tracking reports.
- board or loan committee reports and minutes related to O&G lending activities.
- loans for which terms have been modified by a reduction of the interest rate or principal payment, by a deferral of interest or principal, or by other restructuring of payment terms.
- loans on which interest has been capitalized subsequent to initial underwriting.
- overdisbursed loans.
- loan participations purchased and sold since the previous examination.
- Shared National Credits, if applicable.
- organizational chart of the O&G lending and internal engineering departments.
- résumés of the O&G lending department management and internal engineering staff, to include any additional staff added since the last examination.
- loans to insiders of the bank or any affiliate of the bank.

4. In discussions with bank management, determine if there have been any significant changes in O&G lending (for example, in policies, processes, personnel, control systems, third-party relationships, products, services, delivery channels, volumes, markets, geographies, etc.) since the prior examination. Discussions should address

- management's strategy for the O&G lending function, including
  - growth goals.
  - existing and potential sources of loan demand.
  - new loan types, property types, or geographic regions.
  - new marketing strategies and initiatives.
- the staff's experience and ability to implement strategic initiatives and achieve goals.
- current and projected concentrations of credit, as well as management's plans to manage concentrations.
- significant changes in policies, procedures, underwriting, personnel, and control systems.
- internal or external factors that could affect the portfolio.
- stress testing practices.
- observations from examiner review of internal bank reports, as well as OCC and other third-party-generated reports.
- the extent of syndicated distribution and participation activities as a buyer and a seller, if applicable.

5. Based on an analysis of information obtained in the previous steps, as well as input from the EIC, determine the scope and objectives of the O&G lending examination. Consider

- growth and acquisitions.
- board or management changes.
- changes in risk limits, including concentrations.
- changes in external factors such as
  - national, regional, and local economies.
  - industry outlook.
  - regulatory framework.
  - technological changes.

6. For federal savings associations, determine if O&G loans are approaching the limits described in 12 USC 1464(c) and 12 CFR 160.30. O&G loans typically are classified as commercial loans, which, under 12 USC 1464(c)(2)(A), cannot exceed 20 percent of total assets, provided that commercial loans in excess of 10 percent of assets must be small business loans. Small business loans include any loan to a small business (defined in 13 CFR 121) and any loan that does not exceed $2 million and is for commercial, corporate, business, or agricultural purposes. A federal savings association, however, may make O&G loans under other authority, depending on the circumstances. For example, to the extent an O&G loan is secured by nonresidential real property, a federal savings association may make the loan under its nonresidential loan authority. Under this authority, a federal savings association generally may make loans secured by nonresidential real property up to 400 percent of capital.

Quantity of Risk

Conclusion: The quantity of credit and other associated risks is (low, moderate, or high).

Credit Risk

Objective: To determine the quantity of credit risk associated with O&G production lending. Consider the product mix, markets, geographies, technologies, volumes, size of the exposures, quality metrics, concentrations, etc.

1. Analyze the composition and changes to the O&G portfolio, including off-balance-sheet exposure, since the previous examination. Determine the implications for the quantity of risk of the following:

   - Any significant growth.
   - Material changes in the portfolio, including
     - changes and trends in problem, classified, past-due, non-accrual, and nonperforming assets; charge-off volumes; and risk rating distribution.
     - any significant concentrations.
     - O&G portfolios acquired from other institutions.

2. Assess the effect of external factors, including economic, industry, competitive, and market conditions.

3. Assess the effect of potential legislative, regulatory, accounting, and technological changes.

4. Select a sample of loans to be reviewed. Selection of the sample should be consistent with the examination objectives, supervisory strategy, and district business plans. Refer to the "Sampling Methodologies" booklet of the *Comptroller's Handbook* for guidance on sampling techniques. Consider

   - new, large loans.
   - new loan types.
   - loans originated in new geographic regions or in new O&G producing areas.
   - loans approaching or above the legal lending limit.
   - loans to insiders of the bank or any affiliates.
   - overdisbursed loans.
   - loans with multiple renewals or extensions.
   - special mention loans and classified loans.
   - loans with significant policy or underwriting exceptions.
   - loans with modified repayment terms.

- concentration reports.
- portfolio stress testing reports.

5. Obtain and review credit files for all borrowers in the sample and prepare line sheets for the sampled credits. Line sheets should contain sufficient analysis to determine the credit rating; support any criticisms of underwriting, servicing, or credit administration practices; and document any violations of law. In particular, file readers should

- evaluate the quality of underwriting if the loan was originated, renewed, or restructured in the past 12 months. Consider whether the approval document is consistent with the bank's underwriting policy.
- determine the primary source of repayment of each loan and evaluate its adequacy.
- assess the adequacy of cash flow to meet debt service requirements.
- evaluate the integrity of engineering data.
  - Evaluate support for the assumptions used to determine pricing and the discount rate.
  - Assess the timing of reports to determine if current conditions warrant updates.
- determine if an independent, competent engineer performed the engineering report. If performed by an engineer hired by the borrower, evaluate the review performed by the bank's independent internal or third-party engineer.
- evaluate the borrowing base.
  - Determine the type of reserves that comprises the borrowing base.
  - Assess reliability of past production results used to determine the borrowing base and whether it is sufficient to amortize the debt over a reasonable amount of time and within prudent policy guidelines.
- determine whether appropriate risk factors are used to discount the PWFNI when proved but not producing reserves are used in the borrowing base calculation.
- comment as necessary regarding historical trends in production levels and income to cover operating expenses.
- evaluate budgeted expenses, including the level and trend of capital expenditures, anticipated working capital needs, and costs for any replacement initiatives.
- analyze secondary sources of repayment provided by guarantors, financial sponsors, or endorsers. If the financial condition of the borrower warrants concern, determine the guarantor's, sponsor's, or endorser's capacity and willingness to repay the credit. Review the obligations of these guarantors and consider the likelihood that any or all contingent obligations will be called.
- determine the impact of hedging and when hedging will be required, where applicable.
- evaluate the impact of changes to technology, government regulations, current price levels, or economic markets, where applicable.
- compare collateral with the description on the collateral register.
- determine that property assignments, stock powers, hypothecation agreements, statements of purpose, etc., are on file.
- test the pricing of negotiable collateral, if applicable.

- determine that each file contains documentation supporting guarantees and subordination agreements, where appropriate.
- list all collateral discrepancies and investigate.
- evaluate the due diligence performed to assess environmental risk.
- evaluate sufficiency of collateral coverage. Determine that appraisal and inspections of machinery and equipment are present.
- determine whether the borrower complies with the loan agreement and financial covenants.
- evaluate sensitivity analysis. Assess the impact of changes to the borrower's primary and secondary repayment ability. Compare updates to both the base case and sensitivity case analyses to the standards set in the bank's policy. Determine at what point the stress would cause repayment to fall below the bank's standards and no longer meet policy requirements. Determine the likelihood of such stress event(s).
- document all significant loan policy, loan administration, and underwriting exceptions, and whether the exceptions were appropriately identified, approved, and reported.
- determine any significant structural weaknesses and the impact on the borrower's ability to repay on reasonable terms.
- assign risk ratings to the sampled credits. Refer to risk rating guidance in this booklet and supervisory guidance regarding risk ratings.

6. Review the completed line sheets and summarize the loan sample results. The examiner responsible for the O&G lending review should

   - identify recommended loan risk rating downgrades and ensure such decisions are appropriately documented.
   - maintain a list of structurally weak loans reviewed.
   - maintain a list of loans for which examiners were unable to determine the risk rating due to a lack of information.
   - maintain a list of loans not supported by current and complete financial information and engineering reports, and loans in which collateral documentation is deficient.
   - summarize whether policy, underwriting, loan administration, or documentation exceptions were appropriately identified and approved.

7. Analyze the level, composition, and trend of policy and underwriting exceptions, and determine the impact on the quantity of risk. Consider the frequency of reporting, the total dollar volume, and the percent of the portfolio that exceptions represent in comparison with established limits. (**Note:** A bank's lack of an internal tracking system indicates a need to test for adherence to policy.)

8. Evaluate the trend and level of concentrations as a percentage of total capital. Consider exposure compared to policy limits for individual wells, fields, political or regulatory jurisdictions, extraction technologies, etc.

9. Evaluate portfolio stress testing. Determine whether assumptions to develop base case and downside cases are reasonable and whether key vulnerabilities have been considered.

10. Determine whether any previously charged-off O&G loans have been re-booked.

11. Using a list of non-accruing loans, test loan accrual records to determine that interest income is not being recorded.

12. Evaluate the adequacy of the ALLL for the O&G portfolio.

13. Review the quantity of credit risk indicators in appendix A to this booklet, as appropriate.

14. Discuss the results of the loan sample with the EIC or loan portfolio management (LPM) examiner and bank management.

Other Associated Risks

In addition to credit risk, O&G production lending can generate interest rate risk, liquidity risk, operational risk, compliance risk, strategic risk, and reputation risk. These risks and how O&G production lending can expose the bank to these risks are discussed in the "Introduction" section of this booklet.

Objective: To determine the quantity of other risks associated with O&G production lending activities.

1. Assess the effect of O&G production lending on the quantity of interest rate risk. Consider

   - the effect of interest rate changes on both the borrowers and the bank.
   - underwriting terms such as tenor and management's pricing structure, e.g., fixed vs. variable interest rates and the potential exposure to different pricing indices.
   - off-balance-sheet exposures.
   - the quality and results of sensitivity analysis and portfolio stress testing.

2. Assess the effect of O&G production lending on the quantity of liquidity risk. Consider

   - O&G production portfolio growth rates and the corresponding funding strategies.
   - the composition and trends of the O&G production portfolio and the ability to convert the loans to cash. Consider correlated concentrations of O&G production loans that may be subject to similar supply and demand volatility.
   - current market conditions, including
     - longer-term liquidity pressure due to capped or abandoned wells, reduced exploration, and population migration.
     - deposit trends in regions dependent on the O&G economy.

3. Assess the effect of O&G production lending on the quantity of operational risk. Consider

   - any operational losses resulting from the O&G production lending function.
   - any control weaknesses identified by audit, loan review, or any other risk management or control group.
   - the quality of board oversight.
   - the quality of the loan approval and underwriting process.
   - the quality of credit administration, e.g., segregation of duties, financial analysis, and monitoring and documentation standards.
   - the quality and independence of the engineering function.
   - the quality and independence of the audit and loan review functions.
   - staffing turnover affecting the O&G production function.
   - the quality of and any changes in significant third-party relationships.
   - responses to the internal control questionnaire (ICQ).

4. Assess the effect of O&G production lending on the quantity of compliance risk. Consider

   - the bank's history of compliance with lending-related laws and regulations, particularly those regarding appraisals, insider lending activities, legal lending limits, and affiliates, as well as safe and sound banking practices.
   - for federal savings associations, whether the association is approaching or has exceeded its Home Owners' Loan Act investment limits set forth in 12 USC 1464(c).
   - the quality of the bank's environmental risk management program and losses attributed to liabilities resulting from environmental risk.
   - compliance with internal policies and procedures.

5. Assess the effect of O&G production lending on the level of strategic risk. Consider

   - management's strategy regarding O&G production lending and the potential effect on risk including those posed by concentrations.
   - board oversight of strategic initiatives and stated risk appetite.
   - the adequacy of the bank's program for monitoring economic and market conditions. Consider management's assessment of O&G supply and demand, government policies, and socioeconomic and demographic trends.
   - the ability of the staff to implement O&G production lending strategies without exposing the bank to unwarranted risk.

6. Assess the effect of O&G production lending on the level of reputation risk. Consider

   - the bank's effectiveness in meeting the O&G production needs of the communities it serves, including credit needs of small businesses that depend on the O&G industry.
   - management's oversight of environmental compliance and social responsibility pertaining to O&G lending.

- the volume of syndicated O&G production loans, and the bank's ability to meet its legal or fiduciary responsibilities in sourcing and syndicating O&G production loans.
- management's oversight of complex structured finance arrangements.

Quality of Risk Management

Conclusion: The quality of risk management is (strong, satisfactory, or weak).

The conclusion on risk management considers all risks associated with the bank's O&G production lending activities.

Policies

Policies are statements of actions adopted by a bank to pursue certain objectives. Policies often set standards (on risk tolerances, for example) and should be consistent with the bank's underlying mission, values, and principles. A policy review should always be triggered when the bank's objectives or standards change.

Objective: To determine the adequacy of the O&G loan policies.

1. Assess loan structures permitted and how borrowing base will be determined.

2. Assess maximum advance rates for all categories of O&G reserves.

3. Assess frequency of borrowing base redeterminations (industry standard is semiannually).

4. Assess how borrowing base deficiencies are cured and how long the bank gives the borrower to cure them.

5. Determine minimum percentage of production loan value attributable to PDP reserves.

6. Apply risk adjustments for nonproducing reserves to discount values prior to applying advance rates to the borrowing base.

7. Assess maximum loan term and whether the term reflects the purpose and source of repayment.

8. Determine if there is a periodic review and adjustment, if necessary, of the O&G pricing policy (price deck) assumptions and escalation factors for base case and sensitivity case analyses. Industry standard is to review the O&G pricing policy at least quarterly. Reasoning for changes should be documented in writing. Consider

   - how is the price deck determined?
   - how often is the price deck reviewed (industry standard is at least quarterly)?
   - what is the process for making changes?
   - is the reasoning for changes documented in writing?
   - does the policy address price and expense escalation?

---

9. Assess hedging activities and strategies, including maximum percent of PDP reserves hedged and maximum tenor of hedges.

10. Determine if policy covers documentation and filing requirements.

11. Determine if policy specifies percentage of O&G properties to be covered under mortgage.

12. Determine if there is a comprehensive engineering policy that provides guidelines for engineers, including discount rates applied to future net income to arrive at the PWFNI. Some banks maintain a separate engineering policy.

13. Determine if policy addresses environmental risk.

14. Determine if policy outlines collateral margins for specific types of O&G equipment lending.

15. Determine if policy addresses how O&G loan policy exceptions are defined, identified, monitored, and controlled, including expectations for the frequency of exception report updates. Has the bank established a limit for the percent of the portfolio with exceptions and does it monitor its performance against this limit?

16. Determine how credit enhancements (personal guarantees, hedging, etc.) are used to support credit underwriting.

17. Does the board review and approve the O&G lending policy annually?

    - Does it evaluate existing policies to determine if they are compatible with market conditions?
    - Does it ensure policies are consistent with the bank's strategic direction and risk appetite?

Processes

Processes are the procedures, programs, and practices that impose order on a bank's pursuit of its objectives. Processes define how daily activities are carried out. Effective processes are consistent with the underlying policies and are governed by appropriate checks and balances (such as internal controls).

Objective: To determine the adequacy of the bank's lending practices, procedures, and internal controls regarding O&G loans.

1. Evaluate how policies, procedures, and plans affecting the O&G portfolio are communicated. Consider whether

- management has clearly communicated objectives and risk limits as a percentage of total capital for the O&G portfolio to the board of directors and whether the board has approved these goals.
- communication to key personnel in the O&G department is clear and timely.

2. Assess the process to ensure the accuracy and integrity of the O&G loan data.

- Is there a process to backtest data by comparing production and expenses from previous engineering evaluations to actual production and expenses for the same period?

3. Assess the underwriting process for O&G lending. Consider

- the appropriateness of the approval process, including approval limits of officers.
- the quality of the loan approval documents. Do they contain the following?
    - Industry analysis.
    - Description of the company's operations, including management depth and experience.
    - Comprehensive financial analysis of the borrower and any guarantors, including financial projections.
    - Identification of loan policy exceptions and any mitigating factors.
    - Identification of key risks and any mitigating factors.
    - Purpose of loan.
    - Primary and secondary sources of repayment.
    - Description of collateral and lien status.
    - Environmental risk factors.
    - Property and liability insurance coverage.
    - Borrower's status with state-specific governing authority.
    - Engineering report summary, including a reconciliation of reserve values between borrowing base redeterminations and a comparison of production and expenses from the previous engineering evaluation to actual production and expenses for the same period.
    - Calculation of borrowing base and compliance monitoring requirements, including composition of reserves in the borrowing base (i.e., percentage of PDP used in the borrowing base composition).
    - Minimum number of wells and maximum amount of production from a single well that will be considered in the borrowing base calculation.
    - Analysis of borrower's historical ability to economically replace reserves.
    - Limits or triggers to implement workout or exit strategies.
    - Support for risk grade assigned.
    - Upgrade and downgrade triggers for the lowest pass and problem grades.
- the quality of the engineering reports and the independence of the engineering function.
- the appropriateness of credit structure.

4. Assess the process for approving exceptions.

   • Is there a process to ensure exceptions are appropriately identified before loans are approved?
   • Does the process ensure identified exceptions must be authorized by appropriate approval authority?

5. Evaluate the accuracy and integrity of the internal risk-rating processes. Consider

   • findings from the loan sample.
   • the role of internal loan review.

6. Determine whether there are processes to monitor strategic and business plans for the O&G portfolio. Consider

   • how the O&G portfolio business plans and strategies affect earnings and capital.

7. Assess the process to ensure compliance with applicable laws, rulings, regulations, and environmental guidelines. Consider

   • special state environmental guidelines, if applicable.

8. Evaluate the effectiveness of processes used to monitor collateral. Consider

   • for O&G production loans, is there a process in place to ensure that preparation of in-house engineering reports or review of external reports is consistently completed in a timely manner so that semiannual borrowing base redeterminations are not delayed?
   • for equipment loans, are values updated periodically? Are values provided by personnel or third parties with sufficient expertise when updating values for specialized equipment (drilling equipment, fracking equipment, etc.)?
   • whether the bank has adequate processes to monitor O&G prices.
   • whether drilling rigs and other equipment are periodically inspected. Are inspections performed by technically qualified and competent inspection personnel or third parties?
   • whether the bank has processes to ensure liens on O&G properties are filed and perfected. Is outside counsel required to review documentation prior to loan closing?
   • whether the bank has processes to monitor the adequacy of insurance coverage.

9. The examiner reviewing the O&G lending portfolio should review the LPM examiner's findings to determine whether additional analysis is required for issues related to O&G lending pertaining to

   • problem credit administration.
   • collections.
   • charge-offs.

10. Review the methodology for evaluating and maintaining the ALLL. Consider whether

- the portfolio is analyzed as a separate pool or further segmented by loan type (oil production, gas production, equipment, service) or geographic area.
- the methodology is reasonable based on historical experience and current trends.

11. Verify that the bank has an effective process to periodically evaluate internal controls. (**Note:** The lack of an effective process may require examiners to conduct additional testing. Please refer to the "Internal Control Questionnaire" section of this booklet for details on additional testing.)

Personnel

Personnel are the bank staff and managers who execute or oversee processes. Personnel should be qualified and competent, and should perform appropriately. They should understand the bank's mission, values, principles, policies, and processes. Banks should design compensation programs to attract, develop, and retain qualified personnel. In addition, compensation programs should be structured in a manner that encourages strong risk management practices.

Objective: Given the size and complexity of the bank, determine whether management, lending, and engineering personnel possess and display acceptable knowledge and technical skills to manage and perform their duties.

1. Evaluate the adequacy of the O&G lending staff in terms of the level of expertise and number of assigned personnel. Consider

- whether staffing levels support current operations or any planned growth.
- staff turnover.
- the staff's previous O&G lending and workout experience.
- specialized training provided.
- the average account load per lending officer. Consider reasonableness in light of the complexity and condition of the officer's portfolio.
- how senior management and the board of directors periodically evaluate O&G lenders' understanding of and conformance with the bank's stated credit culture and loan policy. If there is no process, determine the impact on the management of credit risk.

2. Assess the performance management and compensation programs for O&G lending personnel. Consider whether these programs measure and reward behaviors that support strategic and risk appetite objectives for the portfolio.

3. Evaluate the adequacy of the internal engineering staff in terms of the level of expertise and number of assigned personnel. Consider

- whether staffing levels support current operations or any planned growth.

- staff education and experience.
- staff turnover.
- continuing education completed each year.
- succession planning.

4. Assess the independence of the internal engineering function. Consider

- who prepares the annual performance evaluations of the engineers.
- whether that individual also has loan approval authority.
- whether the engineer's overall compensation program includes incentive bonuses for loan volume generated in the bank or department. If so, what percentage of their total compensation do those bonuses represent?

5. If the bank has third-party relationships that involve critical activities, determine whether oversight is consistent with OCC Bulletin 2013-29, "Third-Party Relationships: Risk Management Guidance."

Control Systems

Control systems are the functions (such as internal and external audits, risk review, and quality assurance) and information systems that bank managers use to measure performance, make decisions about risk, and assess the effectiveness of processes. Control functions should have clear reporting lines, adequate resources, and appropriate authority. MIS should provide timely, accurate, and relevant feedback.

Objective: To determine whether the bank has systems in place to provide accurate and timely assessments of the risks associated with its O&G production lending activities.

1. Evaluate the effectiveness of monitoring systems to identify, measure, and track compliance with the O&G policy. Consider

- approval and monitoring of policy limit exceptions, including O&G concentration limits.
- the volume, type and terms of exceptions, including any identified in the loan sample.
- borrower hedging programs.
- internal loan review, audit, and compliance process findings.

2. Determine whether MIS, including engineering reports, provide timely, useful information to evaluate risk levels and trends in the O&G portfolio. For example, is there a worksheet showing key performance and underwriting metrics? Is this information updated at least quarterly and used to monitor the portfolio?

3. Assess the effectiveness of operational controls. Consider

   - segregation of duties.
   - quality control testing and monitoring systems.
   - data reconciliation.
   - system access including logical access and physical access to negotiable items or vaults.

4. Assess the scope, frequency, effectiveness, and independence of the internal and external audits of the O&G production lending function. Consider the qualifications of audit personnel and evaluate accessibility to necessary information and board responses to audit findings.

5. Assess the effectiveness of loan review. Evaluate the scope, frequency, effectiveness, and independence of loan review, as well as their ability to identify and report emerging risks. Determine whether loan review reports address the

   - quality of the O&G production portfolio.
   - trend in portfolio quality.
   - effectiveness of the engineering function.
   - reliability of price deck, price deck assumptions, and updates to the price deck.
   - quality of individual loan and portfolio stress testing.
   - quality of significant relationships.
   - level and trend of policy, underwriting, and pricing exceptions.

Conclusions

Conclusion: The aggregate level of each associated risk is (low, moderate, or high). The direction of each associated risk is (increasing, stable, or decreasing).

Objective: To determine, document, and communicate overall findings and conclusions regarding the examination of O&G production lending.

1. Determine preliminary examination findings and conclusions and discuss with the EIC, including

   - quantity of associated risks (as noted in the "Introduction" section).
   - quality of risk management.
   - aggregate level and direction of associated risks.
   - overall risk in O&G production lending.
   - violations and other concerns.

Summary of Risks Associated with O&G Production Lending				
Risk category	Quantity of risk (Low, moderate, high)	Quality of risk management (Weak, satisfactory, strong)	Aggregate level of risk (Low, moderate, high)	Direction of risk (Increasing, stable, decreasing)
Credit				
Interest rate				
Liquidity				
Operational				
Compliance				
Strategic				
Reputation				

2. If substantive safety and soundness concerns remain unresolved that may have a material adverse effect on the bank, further expand the scope of the examination by completing verification procedures.

3. Discuss examination findings with bank management, including violations, matters requiring attention (MRA), recommendations, and conclusions about risks and risk management practices. If necessary, obtain commitments for corrective action.

4. Compose conclusion comments, highlighting any issues that should be included in the report of examination. If necessary, compose MRA comments.

5. Update the OCC's information system and any applicable report of examination schedules or tables.

6. Write a memorandum specifically setting out what the OCC should do in the future to effectively supervise O&G production lending in the bank, including time periods, staffing, and workdays required.

7. Update, organize, and reference work papers in accordance with OCC policy.

8. Ensure any paper or electronic media that contain sensitive bank or customer information are appropriately disposed of or secured.

Internal Control Questionnaire

An ICQ helps an examiner assess a bank's internal controls for an area. ICQs typically address standard controls that provide day-to-day protection of bank assets and financial records. The examiner decides the extent to which it is necessary to complete or update ICQs during examination planning or after reviewing the findings and conclusions of the core assessment.

Policies

1. Has the board of directors, consistent with its duties and responsibilities, adopted written O&G loan policies that are consistent with safe and sound banking practice and appropriate to the size of the bank and to the nature and scope of its operations? In particular, do the bank's policies

   - identify the geographic areas where the bank will consider lending?
   - establish a loan portfolio diversification policy and set limits as a percentage of total capital for O&G loans by type and geographic market?
   - establish policies for the identification, monitoring, and management of concentrations?
   - identify appropriate terms and conditions for lending on different types of reserves and equipment based on risk?
   - establish loan origination and approval procedures, both generally and by size and type of loan?
   - establish prudent underwriting standards that are clear and measurable, including
     - the maximum loan amount by purpose, and collateral?
     - maximum loan maturities by purpose and collateral?
     - amortization schedules?
     - borrowing base determinations?
     - collateral coverage?

2. Has the bank also established loan administration and documentation expectations for its O&G portfolio that address

   - type and frequency of financial statements, including requirements for verification of information provided by the borrower?
   - type and frequency of engineering reports and updates, including updates to the price deck?
   - type and frequency of collateral evaluations and inspections (appraisals and other estimates of value)?
   - loan closing and disbursement procedures, including the supervised disbursement of proceeds on O&G production loans?
   - payment processing?
   - loan payoffs?
   - delinquency and follow-up procedures?

- foreclosure timing?
- extensions and other forms of forbearance?
- acceptance of deeds in lieu of foreclosure?
- claims processing (e.g., seeking recovery on a defaulted loan covered by an insurance program)?
- servicing and participation agreements?

3. Are procedures in effect to monitor compliance with the bank's O&G lending policies?

   - Are exception loans of a significant size reported individually to the board of directors?
   - Are the numbers, types, and trends of exceptions monitored so that the loan policy and lending practices can be periodically evaluated?
   - Are loans that are in excess of the borrowing base identified?

4. Does the bank effectively monitor conditions in the O&G markets to ensure that the O&G lending policies remain appropriate?

   - Is there a formal process to reconcile reserve values between borrowing base redeterminations?

5. Does the bank's policy or procedures address each O&G lending product offered by the bank and provide guidance for each category, including, for example, oil, natural gas, PUD reserves, PDNP reserves, unproved reserves, and equipment?

6. Does the bank have an internal review procedure to determine whether the engineer consistently follows engineering policies and procedures and that documentation supports those conclusions?

7. Are there policies and procedures to ensure that preparation of in-house engineering reports, or review of external reports, is consistently completed in a timely manner so that semiannual borrowing base redeterminations are not delayed?

8. Are procedures in place to review engineering reports and assumptions for reasonableness before funds are advanced?

9. Does the bank take steps to determine whether there are any environmental hazards associated with the real estate proposed to be mortgaged?

10. When there is reason to believe that there may be serious environmental problems associated with property that it holds as collateral, does the bank

    - take steps to monitor the situation to minimize any potential liability on the part of the bank?
    - seek the advice of experts, particularly in situations where the bank may be considering foreclosure on the contaminated property?

O&G Underwriting

11. Does the bank require

- current and historical financial statements?
- current and historical tax returns?
- credit checks?

12. Do O&G production loan budgets include all costs to bring the hydrocarbons to market both initially and over the life of the loan (including maintenance expenses over that period)?

13. Does the bank require an estimated cost breakdown for each expense?

14. Does the bank require that cost estimates of O&G projects be reviewed by qualified personnel, i.e., independent engineers?

Disbursements

15. Are disbursements

- advanced on a prearranged disbursement plan?
- made only after reviewing independent engineering reports?
- subject to advance, written authorization by the
  - borrower?
  - lending officer?
- reviewed by a bank employee who had no part in granting the loan?
- compared to original cost estimates?
- checked against previous disbursements?
- made directly to suppliers or vendors?
- made in accordance with the loan agreement?

16. Are there periodic reviews of undisbursed loan proceeds to determine their adequacy and that they are reconciled to the budget?

Documentation

17. Does the bank require that documentation files include

- loan applications?
- financial statements for the
  - borrower?
  - guarantors?

- credit and trade checks on the
  - borrower?
  - guarantors?
- copy of all O&G project budgets?
- loan agreement?
- engineering and appraisal reports?
- title searches and other lien searches?
- copies of transfer (or division) orders from the reserve purchaser? (**Note:** Most title opinions verify existence of proper payee on division orders to assist in the determination of ownership [division order title opinion] when title is being transferred from a seller to the buyer. New division orders are issued to the new owner from a certified copy of a filed assignment or deed of trust.)
- mortgage?
- financing statements and security agreements?
- disbursement authorizations?
- insurance policies?
- hedging contracts or commitments?

Conclusion

18. Is the foregoing information an adequate basis for evaluating internal controls in that there are no significant additional internal auditing procedures, accounting controls, administrative controls, or other circumstances that impair any controls or mitigate any weaknesses indicated above (explain negative answers briefly and indicate conclusions as to their effect on specific examination or verification procedures)?

19. Based on the answers to the foregoing questions, internal controls for O&G lending are considered (strong, satisfactory, weak).

Verification Procedures

Verification procedures are used to verify the existence of assets and liabilities, or test the reliability of financial records. Examiners generally do not perform verification procedures as part of a typical examination. Rather, verification procedures are performed when substantive safety and soundness concerns are identified that are not mitigated by the bank's risk management systems and internal controls.

1. Reconcile the trial balance to the general ledger. Include loan commitments, overdrafts, and other contingent liabilities in the testing.

2. Using an appropriate sampling technique, select loans from the trial balance and

    *   prepare and mail confirmation forms to borrowers. (Loans serviced by other institutions, either whole loans or participations, should be confirmed only with the servicing institution. Loans serviced for other institutions, either whole loans or participations, should be confirmed with the other institution and the borrower. Confirmation forms should include the borrower's name, loan number, original amount, interest rate, current loan balance, contingency and escrow account balance, and a brief description of the collateral.)
        *   After a reasonable time, mail second requests.
        *   Follow up on any no-replies or exceptions and resolve differences.
    *   examine notes for completeness and reconcile date, amount, and terms to trial balance.
        *   If any notes are not held at the bank, request confirmation with the holder.
        *   See that required initials of approving officer are on the note.
        *   See that the note is signed, appears to be genuine, and is negotiable.
    *   compare collateral held in files with the description on the collateral register. List and investigate all collateral discrepancies.
    *   determine if any collateral is held by an outside custodian or has been temporarily removed for any reason. Request confirmation for any collateral held outside the bank.
    *   determine that each file contains documentation supporting guarantees and subordination agreements, where appropriate.
    *   determine that any required insurance coverage is adequate and that the bank is named as loss payee.
    *   review participation agreements making excerpts, when deemed necessary, for such items as rate of service fee, interest rate, retention of late charges, and remittance requirements, and determine whether the customer has complied.
    *   review loan agreement provisions for holdback or retention, and determine if undisbursed loan funds or contingency or escrow accounts are equal to retention or holdback requirements.
        *   If separate reserves are maintained, determine if debit entries to those accounts are authorized in accordance with the terms of the loan agreement and if they are supported by inspection reports, individual bills, or other evidence.

- review disbursement ledgers and authorizations, and determine if authorizations are signed in accordance with the terms of the loan agreement.
- reconcile debits in the undisbursed loan proceeds accounts to inspection reports, individual bills, or other evidence supporting disbursements.

3. Review the accrued interest accounts and

- review procedures for accounting for accrued interest and handling of adjustments.
- scan accrued interest and income accounts for any unusual entries and follow up on any unusual items by tracing to initial and supporting records.

4. Obtain or prepare a schedule showing the amount of monthly interest income and balances at the end of each month since the last examination and

- calculate or check yield.
- investigate significant fluctuations or trends.

5. Using a list of non-accruing loans, check loan accrual records to determine that interest income is not being accrued and whether cash payments received are applied to principal when collection is in doubt.

Appendixes

Appendix A: Quantity of Credit Risk Indicators

Examiners should consider the following indicators when assessing the quantity of credit risk of O&G production lending activities.

Low	Moderate	High
The level of O&G loans outstanding is low relative to capital.	The level of O&G loans outstanding is moderate relative to capital.	The level of O&G loans outstanding is high relative to capital.
O&G growth rates are supported by local, regional, or national economic trends. Growth, including off-balance-sheet activities, has been planned for and is commensurate with management and staff expertise, as well as operational capabilities.	O&G growth rates exceed local, regional, or national economic trends. Growth, including off-balance-sheet activities, has not been planned for or exceeds planned levels and may test the capabilities of management, credit staff, and MIS.	O&G growth rates significantly exceed local, regional, or national economic trends. Growth, including off-balance-sheet activities, has not been planned for or exceeds planned levels and stretches the experience and capability of management, credit staff, and MIS. Growth may also be in new products or outside the bank's traditional lending area.
Interest and fee income from O&G lending activities is not a significant portion of loan income.	Interest and fee income from O&G lending activities is an important component of loan income; the bank's lending activities, however, remain diversified.	The bank is highly dependent on interest and fees from O&G lending activities. Management may seek higher returns through higher risk product or customer types. Loan yields may be insufficient relative to risk.
The bank's O&G portfolio is well diversified with no single large concentrations or a few moderate concentrations. Concentrations are well within reasonable internal limits. The O&G portfolio mix does not materially affect the risk profile.	The bank has a few material O&G concentrations that may be approaching internal limits. The O&G portfolio mix may increase the bank's credit risk profile.	The bank has large O&G concentrations that may exceed internal limits. The O&G portfolio mix increases the bank's credit risk profile.
O&G underwriting is conservative. Policies and procedures are reasonable. O&G loans with structural weaknesses or underwriting exceptions are occasionally originated; the weaknesses, however, are effectively mitigated.	O&G underwriting is satisfactory. The bank has an average level of O&G loans with structural weaknesses. Exceptions are reasonably mitigated and consistent with competitive pressures and reasonable growth objectives.	O&G underwriting is liberal, and policies are inadequate. The bank has a high level of O&G loans with structural weaknesses or underwriting exceptions, the volume of which exposes the bank to loss in the event of default.

Low	Moderate	High
Collateral requirements for O&G loans are conservative. Collateral valuations are reasonable, timely, and well supported.	Collateral requirements for O&G loans are acceptable. Some collateral exceptions exist, but they are reasonably mitigated and monitored. A moderate volume of collateral valuations is not well supported. Updated collateral valuations are not always obtained in a timely manner.	Collateral requirements for O&G loans are liberal, or if policies are conservative, substantial deviations exist. Collateral valuations are not always obtained, are frequently unsupported, or reflect inadequate protection. Updated collateral values are not obtained in a timely manner.
The level of O&G loan documentation or collateral exceptions are low and have minimal impact on the bank's risk profile.	The level of O&G loan documentation or collateral exceptions is moderate; exceptions, however, are reasonably mitigated and corrected in a timely manner, if applicable. The risk of loss from these exceptions is not material.	The level of O&G loan documentation or collateral exceptions is high. Exceptions are not mitigated and not corrected in a timely manner. The risk of loss from the exceptions is heightened.
O&G loan distribution across pass category is consistent with a conservative risk appetite. Migration trends within pass category favor the less risky ratings. Lagging indicators, including past dues and nonaccruals, are low and stable.	O&G distribution across pass category is consistent with a moderate risk appetite. Migration trends within pass category may favor riskier ratings. Lagging indicators, including past dues and nonaccruals, are moderate and may be slightly increasing.	O&G distribution across pass category is heavily skewed toward riskier pass ratings. Lagging indicators, including past dues and nonaccruals, are moderate or high, and the trend is increasing.
The volume of classified and special mention O&G loans is low and is not skewed toward more severe risk ratings.	The volume of classified and special mention O&G loans is moderate but is not skewed toward more severe ratings.	The volume of classified and special mention O&G loans is moderate or high, skewed to the more severe ratings, and increasing.
O&G refinancing and renewal practices raise little or no concern regarding the quality of O&G loans and the accuracy of reported problem loan data.	O&G refinancing and renewal practices pose some concern regarding the quality of O&G loans and the accuracy of reported problem loan data.	O&G refinance and renewal practices raise substantial concerns regarding the quality of O&G loans and the accuracy of reported problem loan data.
The volume of O&G loans with environmental issues is not significant. Environmental analyses are timely, appropriate, and well supported.	A moderate volume of O&G loans with environmental concerns exists; the risks, however, are identified and reasonably mitigated. Environmental evaluations are not always performed in a timely manner.	The volume of O&G loans with environmental concerns is material if left uncorrected. Environmental evaluations are not performed in a timely manner, or management's response to identified environmental issues is not appropriate.

Appendix B: Quality of Credit Risk Management Indicators

Examiners should consider the following indicators when assessing the quality of credit risk management of O&G production lending activities.

Strong	Satisfactory	Weak
There is a clear, sound O&G credit culture. Board and management's appetite for risk is well communicated and fully understood.	The O&G credit culture is generally sound, but the culture may not be uniform and risk appetite may not be clearly communicated throughout the bank.	The O&G credit culture is absent or materially flawed. Risk appetite may not be well understood.
O&G initiatives are consistent with a conservative risk appetite and promote an appropriate balance between risk taking and strategic objectives. New O&G loan products are well researched, tested, and approved before implementation.	O&G initiatives are consistent with a moderate risk profile. Generally, there is an appropriate balance between risk taking and strategic objectives; anxiety for income, however, may lead to higher risk transactions. New O&G products may be launched without sufficient testing, but risks are generally understood.	O&G initiatives are liberal and encourage risk taking. Anxiety for income dominates planning activities. The bank introduces new O&G products without conducting sufficient due diligence.
Management is effective. The O&G lending and engineering staffs possess sufficient expertise to effectively administer the risk assumed. Responsibilities and accountability are clear, and appropriate remedial or corrective action is taken when risk limits are breached.	O&G risk management is satisfactory, but improvement may be needed in one or more areas. O&G lending and engineering staff generally possess the expertise to administer assumed risks; additional expertise, however, may be required. Responsibilities and accountability may require some clarification. In general, appropriate remedial or corrective action is taken when risk limits are breached.	O&G risk management is deficient. O&G lending and engineering staff may not possess sufficient expertise or may demonstrate an unwillingness to effectively administer the risk assumed. Responsibilities and accountability may not be clear. Corrective actions are insufficient to address root causes of problems.
Diversification management is effective. O&G concentration limits are set at reasonable levels. O&G concentration risk management practices are sound, including management's efforts to reduce or mitigate exposures. Management effectively identifies and understands correlated risk exposures and their potential impact.	Diversification management is adequate, but certain aspects may need improvement. O&G concentrations are identified and reported, but limits and other action triggers may be absent or moderately high. Concentration management efforts may be focused at the individual loan level, while portfolio-level efforts may be inadequate. Correlated exposures may not be identified and their risks not fully understood.	Diversification management is passive or deficient. Management may not identify concentrations or take little or no action to reduce, limit, or mitigate the associated risk. Limits may be present but represent a significant portion of capital. Management may not understand exposure correlations and their potential impact. Concentration limits may be exceeded or raised frequently.

Strong	Satisfactory	Weak
Loan management and personnel compensation structures provide appropriate balance among loan/revenue production, loan quality, and portfolio administration, including risk identification.	Loan management and personnel compensation structures provide reasonable balance among loan/revenue production, loan quality, and portfolio administration.	Loan management and personnel compensation structures are skewed to loan/revenue production. There is little evidence of substantive incentives or accountability for loan quality and portfolio administration.
O&G staffing levels and expertise are appropriate for the size and complexity of O&G activities. Staff turnover is low, and the transfer of responsibilities is orderly. Training programs facilitate ongoing staff development.	O&G staffing levels and expertise are generally adequate for the size and complexity of the O&G activities. Staff turnover is moderate and may result in some temporary gaps in portfolio management. Training initiatives are adequate.	O&G staffing levels and expertise are deficient. Turnover is high. Management does not provide sufficient resources for staff training.
O&G lending policies effectively establish and communicate portfolio objectives, risk limits, loan underwriting standards, and risk-selection standards.	O&G lending policies are fundamentally adequate. Enhancement, while generally not critical, can be achieved in one or more areas. Specificity of risk limits or underwriting standards may need improvement to fully communicate policy requirements.	O&G lending policies are deficient in one or more ways and require significant improvements. Policies may not be clear or are too general to adequately communicate portfolio objectives, risk limits, and underwriting and risk-selection standards.
Staff effectively identifies, approves, tracks, and reports significant policy, underwriting, and risk-selection exceptions individually and in aggregate, including risk exposures associated with off-balance-sheet activities.	Staff identifies, approves, and reports significant policy, underwriting, and risk-selection exceptions on a loan-by-loan basis, including risk exposures associated with off-balance-sheet activities. Little aggregation or trend analysis, however, is conducted to determine the effect on portfolio quality.	Staff approves significant policy exceptions but does not report them individually or in aggregate, or does not analyze their effect on portfolio quality. Risk exposures associated with off-balance-sheet activities may not be considered. Policy exceptions may not receive appropriate approval.
Credit analysis is thorough and timely both at underwriting and periodically thereafter.	Credit analysis appropriately identifies key risks and is conducted within reasonable time frames. Monitoring may need improvement.	Credit analysis is deficient. Analysis is superficial, and key risks are overlooked. Credit data are not reviewed in a timely manner.
Risk rating and problem loan review and identification systems are accurate and timely. Credit risk is effectively stratified for both problem and pass rated credits. Systems serve as effective early warning tools and support risk-based pricing, ALLL, and capital allocations.	Risk rating and problem loan review and identification systems are adequate. Problem and emerging problem credits are adequately identified, although room for improvement exists. The graduation of pass ratings may need to be expanded to facilitate early warning, risk-based pricing, or capital allocations.	Risk rating and problem loan review and identification systems are deficient. Problem credits may not be identified accurately or in a timely manner, resulting in misstated levels of portfolio risk. The graduation of pass ratings is insufficient to stratify risk in pass credits for early warning or other purposes.
Special mention ratings do not indicate any issues regarding administration of the O&G portfolio.	Special mention ratings generally do not indicate administration issues within the O&G portfolio.	Special mention ratings indicate management is not properly administering the O&G portfolio.

Strong	**Satisfactory**	**Weak**
MIS provide accurate, timely, and complete O&G portfolio information. Management and the board receive appropriate reports to analyze and understand the impact of O&G activities on the bank's credit risk profile, including off-balance-sheet activities. MIS facilitate timely exception reporting.	Management and the board generally receive appropriate reports to analyze and understand the impact of O&G activities on the bank's credit risk profile; modest improvement, however, may be needed in one or more areas. MIS facilitate generally timely exception reporting.	MIS are deficient. The accuracy or timeliness of information may be affected in a material way. Management and the board may not be receiving sufficient information to analyze and understand the impact of O&G activities on the credit risk profile of the bank. Exception reporting requires improvement.

Appendix C: Glossary

Abandon: (1) The proper plugging and abandoning of a well in compliance with all applicable regulations, and the cleaning up of the well site to the satisfaction of any governmental body having jurisdiction with respect thereto and to the reasonable satisfaction of the operator. (2) To cease completion of a well and salvage drilling or well material and equipment.

Abatement: (1) The act or process of reducing the intensity of pollution. (2) The use of some method of abating pollution.

American Petroleum Institute (API): The American Petroleum Institute is the primary trade association representing the O&G industry in the United States.

Annulus: The space between (1) the casing and the wall of the borehole, (2) two strings of casing, and (3) tubing and casing.

Appraisal well: A well drilled as part of an appraisal drilling program that is carried out to determine the physical extent, reserves, and likely production rate of a field.

Backwardation: Sometimes referred to as normal backwardation. A theory that as a futures contract approaches expiration, the trading price increases.

Barrel, bbl: One barrel of oil (1 barrel = 42 U.S. gallons [approx.] or 35 imperial gallons [approx.] or 159 liters [approx.]; 7.45 barrels = 1 ton [approx.]; 6.29 barrels = 1 cubic meter).

Bcf: Billion cubic feet (1 billion cubic feet of natural gas = .026 million metric tons or 0.18 million barrels of oil equivalent).

Bcm: Billion cubic meters (1 cubic meter = 35.31 cubic feet).

Blow-out: When well pressure exceeds the ability of the wellhead valves to control it. O&G "blow wild" at the surface.

BOE: Barrel of oil equivalent. A unit of measure to equate O&G volumes. Each barrel of oil equals 6,000 cubic feet (or 6 mcf) of natural gas. For example, if a company produces 1 million barrels of oil and 6 million mcf of gas, it has produced 2 million BOE.

Borehole: The hole as drilled by the drill bit.

Borrowing base: A collateral base agreed to by the borrower and lender that is used to limit the amount of funds the lender advances the borrower. The borrowing base specifies the maximum amount that can be borrowed in terms of collateral type, eligibility, and advance rates.

Brownfield production: An existing field that is brought back into production due to improved markets, technology, etc.

Casing: Pipe cemented in the well to seal off formation fluids or keep the hole from caving in. Casing remains in the well as a permanent reinforcement after the drilling is complete.

Completion: The installation of permanent wellhead equipment for the production of O&G.

Condensate: Hydrocarbons that are in the gaseous state under reservoir conditions and become liquid when temperature or pressure is reduced.

Contango: A circumstance in which the futures price of a commodity has risen above the futures spot price. A contango implies that investors are willing to pay a premium for delivery of a commodity in the future rather than pay the carrying costs of buying the commodity today and holding it.

Core: A cylindrical sample of a formation penetrated in a rotary drilling operation. Samples are examined to obtain geological information.

Crude oil: Liquid petroleum as it comes out of the ground as distinguished from refined oils manufactured out of it.

Day rate: The rate paid to a drilling contractor for each day's work under a day work contract, which stipulates that the contractor be paid based on time worked, not footage drilled.

Derrick: The tower-like structure that houses most of the drilling controls.

Development well: Any well drilled in an area where oil or gas has previously been found.

Drilling: The use of a rig and crew for the drilling, suspension, completion, production testing, capping, plugging, and abandoning of a well or the converting of a well to a producing well. Also includes any related environmental studies. Associated costs include completion costs but do not include equipping costs.

Drilling rig: A drilling unit that is not permanently fixed to the seabed, e.g., a drill ship, a semisubmersible, or a jack-up unit. Also means a derrick and its associated machinery.

Dry hole: A well that contains no oil or gas, or too little of either to make production economically viable.

Enhanced oil recovery: A process whereby oil is recovered other than by the natural pressure in a reservoir. Examples include water flooding, use of surfactants, in situ combustion, etc.

Exploration well: A deep hole drilled into the earth by an O&G company that is used to identify new sources of O&G.

Farm in: When a company acquires an interest in an acreage by taking over all or part of the financial commitment for drilling an exploration well.

Fishing: Retrieving objects from the borehole, such as a broken drill string or tools.

Frack boat: An offshore vessel used in offshore frack jobs. These vessels include various tanks, storage compartments, engines, pumps, mixing blenders, etc., for such jobs and coiled tubing that are lowered into the wellbore to provide the frack fluid mix directly into the wellbore.

Fracturing: A method of breaking down a formation by pumping a mixture of fluid, biocide, and proppant(s) under pressure into the formation. The objective is to increase production rates from a reservoir. This method is also referred to as hydraulic fracturing, fluid injection, and fracking.

Future net revenue half-life: The remaining value of cash flow after the depletion of half of the reserves.

Greenfield production: New producing wells operating in a field that has not been in production for a long time.

Ground lease: A lease agreement that allows a tenant to develop the property for the lease period but forfeits rights to the improvements to the property owner when the lease has matured.

Horizontal drilling: A drilling method whereby a vertical drilling hole is redirected so it is parallel to the oil formation, which can then be penetrated from the top.

Hydrocarbon: A compound containing only the elements hydrogen and carbon. May exist as a solid, a liquid, or a gas. The term is mainly used in a catchall sense for oil, gas, and condensate.

Jack-up rig: A mobile offshore drilling rig with legs lowered to the ocean floor as an anchor. Once the legs hit bottom, the body of the rig is "jacked up" above the surface of the water. These rigs are used in shallower applications for drilling, workover, or completion.

Lifting costs: The cost of producing oil or gas from a well or lease.

Liquefied: Light hydrocarbon material, gaseous at atmospheric temperature and pressure, held in the liquid state by pressure to facilitate storage, transport, and handling. Commercial liquefied gas consists essentially of either propane or butane, or a mixture of the two.

Majors: A term referring to the largest multinational integrated oil companies.

Mcf: One thousand cubic feet. The standard measure of natural gas volume (1 mcf = 1 million BTU of energy at 1 atmosphere of pressure; 6 mcf = 1 barrel of oil equivalent [BOE]).

Offset well: A well drilled near other wells to assess the extent and characteristics of the reservoir. In some cases, this type of well is used to drain hydrocarbons from an adjoining lease or tract.

Operator: The company with the legal authority to drill wells and undertake the production of hydrocarbons that are found. The operator is often part of a consortium and acts on behalf of this consortium.

Permeability: The property of a rock formation that quantifies the flow of a fluid through the pore spaces and into the wellbore. A tight rock formation has low permeability and lower capacity to flow O&G. Wells in such formations typically require additional stimulation via fracking or other techniques.

Petroleum gas mud: Often referred to as drilling mud, it is a mixture of base substance and additives used to lubricate the drill bit and counteract the natural pressure of the formation.

Porosity: Refers to the pore space present in the underground formation that enables the rocks composing the formation to hold fluids.

Possible reserves: Unproved reserves that at present cannot be regarded as "probable" due to a low probability of profitable development. The industry standard probability that these reserves are technically and economically producible is 10 percent (or moderately higher).

Primary recovery: Recovery of oil or gas from a reservoir purely by using the natural pressure in the reservoir to force the oil or gas out.

Probable reserves: Unproved reserves that are estimated to have a better than 50 percent chance of being technically and economically producible.

Proved field: An oil or gas field whose physical extent and estimated reserves have been determined.

Proved reserves: Those reserves that on the available evidence are virtually certain to be technically and economically producible (i.e., have a better than 90 percent chance of being produced).

Recoverable reserves: That proportion of the O&G in a reservoir that can be removed using currently available techniques.

Redetermination: Reassessment (repricing) of the borrowing base.

Reservoir: The underground formation where O&G has accumulated. It consists of a porous rock to hold the oil or gas, and a cap rock that prevents its escape.

Rig count: A survey revealing the number of drilling rigs in use during a particular period of time in a given market. Usually includes onshore and offshore rigs, unless specified otherwise.

Rotary drilling: A drilling system in which a rotating bit connected to a hollow drill pipe penetrates a rock formation. Fluid is pumped through the pipe so the rock cuttings can be brought to the surface.

Roughneck: Drill crew members who work on the derrick floor, screwing together the sections of drill pipe when running or pulling a drill string.

Roustabout: Drill crew members who handle the loading and unloading of equipment and assist in general operations around the rig.

Royalty payment: The cash or kind paid to the landowner or holder of royalty rights for a portion of the property's gross production of O&G. Although lease terms vary, a fairly common royalty is one-eighth of production.

Secondary recovery: Recovery of oil or gas from a reservoir by artificially maintaining or enhancing the reservoir pressure by injection of gas, water, or other substances into the reservoir rock. Secondary recovery techniques are used once natural pressure in the well no longer produces free flowing oil or pumping no longer is economically viable.

Semisubmersible rig: A mobile offshore drilling rig that floats partially submerged.

Shut-in well: A well that is capable of producing but is not presently operating. Reasons why a well may be shut in include lack of equipment or market.

Stripper well: A well that makes a nominal volume of production each day, typically 10 bbls or less. Smaller independents sometimes acquire stripper wells and rework them to enhance production.

Submersible rig: A mobile offshore drilling rig with compartments that are flooded to cause the structure to submerge and rest on the seafloor; used in shallow water.

Turnkey contract: A drilling contract that calls for the completion of a well for a fixed price. All costs, including those that are unexpected, must be borne by the drilling contractor.

Utilization rate: The proportion of the total available rig fleet that is active at a given time. Computed by dividing the number of active rigs by the number of available rigs. Differences of opinion regarding the classification of "active" and "available" rigs mean that utilization rates reported by different sources may vary widely. In the marine industry, the percentage use rate for oilfield-related vessels.

Volumetric calculations: A method of determining O&G reserves by use of rock volume and rock characteristics.

Well log: A record of geological formation penetrated during drilling, including technical details of the operation.

Wildcat well: A well drilled in an unproved area. Also known as an "exploration well."

Working interest: The term, also called an operating interest, is used to describe the lease owner's interest in the well. Lease owners pay 100 percent of cost and receive all revenues after taxes and royalties are paid.

Workover: Remedial work to the equipment within a well, the well pipework, or relating to attempts to increase the rate of flow of a well.

Appendix D: Abbreviations

ALLL   allowance for loan and lease losses

API   American Petroleum Institute

BBL   barrel

BTU   British thermal unit

E&P   exploration and production

EIC   examiner-in-charge

GFC   global financial condition

ICQ   internal control questionnaire

LNG   liquefied natural gas

LPM   loan portfolio management

MIS   management information systems

MRA   matters requiring attention

OCC   Office of the Comptroller of the Currency

O&G   oil and natural gas

PDNP   proved developed reserves subcategorized as nonproducing

PDP   proved developed reserves subcategorized as producing

PDSI   proved developed shut in

PUD   proved undeveloped

PWFNI   present worth of future net income

UCC   Uniform Commercial Code

VPP   volumetric production payment

WTI   West Texas Intermediate

References

Laws

12 USC 24, "Corporate Powers of Associations" (national banks)
12 USC 29, "Real Property" (national banks)
12 USC 84, "Lending Limits" (national banks and federal savings associations)
12 USC 1464, "Federal Savings Associations" (federal savings associations)

Regulations

12 CFR 32, "Lending Limits" (national banks and federal savings associations)
12 CFR 34, "Real Estate Lending and Appraisals" (national banks)
12 CFR 160, "Lending and Investment" (federal savings associations)
12 CFR 164, "Appraisals" (federal savings associations)
13 CFR 121, "Small Business Size Regulations" (federal savings associations)

Comptroller's Handbook

Examination Process
"Bank Supervision Process"
"Community Bank Supervision"
"Federal Branches and Agencies Supervision"
"Large Bank Supervision"
"Sampling Methodologies"

Safety and Soundness, Asset Quality
"Allowance for Loan and Lease Losses"
"Concentrations of Credit"
"Loan Portfolio Management"
"Rating Credit Risk"

OCC Issuances

Interpretive Letter 1117 (May 19, 2009) (national banks)
OCC Bulletin 2007-1, "Complex Structured Finance Transactions: Notice of Final Interagency Statement" (January 5, 2007)
OCC Bulletin 2013-29, "Third-Party Relationships: Risk Management Guidance" (October 30, 2013)